The Ultimate Guide to Female Teams

Doc Robyn Odegaard

Stop The Drama! The Ultimate Guide to Female Teams

ISBN 978-0-9846581-0-7

Disclaimer

This book is designed to provide information in regard to the subject matter covered. It is sold or provided with the understanding that the publisher, author, editor, and/or sponsor shall not be held liable in any degree for any loss or injury due to any omission, error, misprinting, or ambiguity. The publisher, author, and editor disclaim any personal liability, directly or indirectly, for advice or information presented within.

Published by Champion Performance Development
www.ChampPerformance.com
www.StopTheDramaNow.com

Edited by & interior designed by Kathryn Marion
www.AuthorsDoula.com

Cover design by Jay Urbaniak
www.EpicFilms.com

Printed in the United States of America

Praise for *Stop The Drama!*

"As a leader in my field, I can most definitely say that Doc Robyn is a leader in hers. The *Stop The Drama!* campaign is innovative and engaging for athletes, their coaches, parents, and team administrators. I firmly believe anyone involved with athletes at any level will benefit by reading this book. It should be required reading for all of the coaches and parents in my league."

Doug Warner, Travel Vice President Youth Soccer,
Piscataway, New Jersey

"Doc Robyn had been doing her amazing work with our team for about a year when I started working with her individually. She helped me understand that how I was communicating with myself was limiting my performance. The skills Doc Robyn provided to me and my team were priceless *and* timeless. I shared them with my family and we are now closer than we have ever been. You cannot go wrong with Doc Robyn and the *Stop The Drama!* campaign. In fact, the only risk you have is NOT grabbing the opportunity with both hands!"

Erin Saunders, Division I diver 2006-2010, Communications Coordinator for the
PA Institute for Instructional Coaching

"I brought Doc Robyn in to work with our team because I knew we had the potential to be much better than our record showed. Our team was not working together as well as they could. By implementing *The Nine Secrets to Great Teamwork* and *The Seven No-Fail Secrets to Stop The Drama!* our players learned how to communicate quickly and effectively both on and off the field. What I didn't expect was how much my staff and I would learn from Doc Robyn, too. Getting the team involved with the *Stop The Drama!* campaign was one of the best coaching decisions I have ever made."

Liz Tchou, Head Coach, Rutgers field hockey

"Doc Robyn's *Stop The Drama!* campaign is applicable from the sports arena to the classroom and beyond to the professional world of work. The drama that exists in the career world is debilitating and energy-depleting, so I am thrilled that Doc Robyn is able to address these issues with practical solutions that will help our young women be more successful, confident, and empowered as they emerge into their career roles. I work with law students in addition to career counseling for adults in my private practice, and the catty drama is rampant and destructive. Doc Robyn's book will be a regular on my "must-read" list for students and professionals. Cheers to her for addressing this most important facet of communication and professional co-existence with action steps that work."

Caroline Dowd-Higgins, Director of Career & Professional Development and Adjunct Faculty
Indiana University Maurer School of Law, Bloomington, IN

"As a former champion athlete and coach, I found Doc Robyn's book, *Stop The Drama!,* to be wonderful. This is not an academic tome. It is written from Doc Robyn's personal experience in the trenches as an athlete, a coach, and a coach's coach and also from her perspective as a behavioral researcher. This book is a breakthrough that contains straightforward, easy-to-apply guidelines and steps that any individual, coach, or parent can take, particularly her *Nine Secrets of Great Teamwork* and her *Seven No-Fail Secrets to Stop The Drama!* And just because Doc Robyn's work has been mainly with female teams, don't for a moment think her message doesn't apply to you fellows—I saw tremendous benefit in her work for males as well."

Roger E. Boswarva, Chairman & Founding Partner,
Ability Consultants, Inc. www.howtolearneasily.com

"Gossip was an understatement when it came to our team. We let the petty things get in the way of everything, including our play. Doc Robyn made us aware that the way we communicated mattered. Her *Seven No-Fail Secrets to Stop The Drama!* gave us the confidence to confront each other using productive conflict. After working with Doc Robyn, we communicated face to face, instead of behind each other's backs. Doc Robyn made a huge positive difference for us. It is my wish that every young woman is afforded the opportunity to learn the life changing skills the *Stop The Drama!* campaign provides."

Kiki Johnson, former D-1 athlete, head JV field hockey coach
Princeton Day School and founder of "Think You're Fancy?"

"When I met Doc Robyn, I knew from our work with female athletes that drama was a problem, but once I became aware of how frequently the drama happens and how it hurts the team, friendships, and individuals, the need to *Stop The Drama!* became much clearer. Reading this book will help you, and experiencing the changes from Doc Robyn's work could be transformational."

Mark Halpert Co-Director 3D Learner Sports Performance

"As a parent, I only want what is best for my children. When my college athlete daughter was experiencing negativity and drama on her team, I was relieved to hear that someone was stepping in to help. That person was Doc Robyn Odegaard. Doc Robyn implemented strategies from her *Stop The Drama!* campaign to educate my daughter and her teammates on how to communicate without drama, backstabbing, and gossip. I have seen a positive difference, not only in how empowered and respectful my daughter is, but in her team and coaching staff as well. The benefits she received from Doc Robyn will continue to contribute to her success for the rest of her life."

Maddie Sands, Parent

"*Stop The Drama!* is so easy to read! When I was first told to read it, I thought it was going to be dry like a textbook. But it is actually fun and I love that I can read just the sections that apply to me. The stories are great and I learned a lot I didn't know."

Melody Young, student, age 21

"I had the opportunity to have Doc Robyn on my radio program and discuss *The Nine Secrets to Great Teamwork* and *The Seven No-Fail Secrets to Stop The Drama!* in depth. I realized how applicable these points are to family communication. After all, a family is a team. I wish my family had operated on these Secrets. I would have felt more supported and therefore closer to my parents and siblings. I also would have learned *critical social skills* that would've helped me succeed in life. *The Seven No-Fail Secrets to Stop The Drama!* and *The Nine Secrets to Great Teamwork* <u>are a must</u> for teaching anyone critical social skills needed to succeed in life."

Virginia Koenig, Founding President, International Society for Performance Improvement, New York Environs Chapter and Author of *How to Learn-How to Teach; Overcoming the Seven Barriers to Comprehension* www.howtolearneasily.com

Table of Contents

Preface

Nice Girl Syndrome

"Nice girls don't argue." "Nice girls don't cause conflict." "Nice girls are friendly." That is what we teach young women. From the time they are babies, they are told how cute and sweet they are. That gets translated into, "Nice girls never say something mean to someone's face; far better to say it behind their back." Why do we, as a culture, allow emotional bullying to be an acceptable way to handle disagreements? All it does is create a firestorm of gossip among people who were not, and should not be, involved in the problem. Yet that is what we are teaching young women, generation after generation.

Breaking the Cycle of Drama

I was told recently about a scientific study where male crabs were put into a jar and it was observed how they worked together to pull each other out. Female crabs in the same jar pulled each other down and never got out. *We are smarter than crabs.* We are failing young women by not teaching them how to work together—that they don't have to tear each other down in order to get ahead.

Young women are not being provided the skills to deal with conflict in a productive way. They aren't taught the communication skills they need to be able to have tough conversations, work through an issue, and move on. They aren't held accountable to owning their feelings about a situation and speaking directly to the person with whom they have an issue.

Sadly, the negative communication of cattiness and drama is encouraged and glorified on reality TV. This doesn't serve women well in college and it isn't doing them any favors in the corporate world. Young women need a new set of communication skills to transform the way they handle conflict.

To break the cycle of using drama to deal with conflict, young women need to understand the process of developing a team communication fingerprint, addressing existing issues, agreeing on how to work through problems in the future and how to hold each other accountable (to not use gossip, backstabbing and catty behavior). It isn't easy, but it *is* possible. In this book, you are going to find tips, ideas, and thought-starters to help you do just that: *Stop The Drama*!

Introduction

A twenty-year-old student-athlete came to my office and sat down across from me to talk. I waited patiently, watching her hands in her lap, tears spilling down her cheeks. She took a deep breath, "He told me to swim more like a *man*... and... <sob> and when I said I didn't know what that meant, he showed me video of Michael Phelps!"

Her voice escalated as she looked at me, hurt and angry, and grabbed the tissues from the desk. "I still don't know what that means! How can I swim like a *man*?! I'm not a man; I can't swim like a man; and it's *stupid* to tell me I should!"

I agreed with her, but I couldn't tell her so. What technique was her coach trying to convey? I knew he had good intentions—he wanted to help her swim fast—but, clearly, communications had broken down.

* * *

Two captains of the team I was scheduled to see the next day stopped me in a parking lot. I tried to understand the huge team blowup they were explaining:

"Kathy (a senior) dated a guy kinda seriously about three years ago. It was crazy hard for her when they broke up."

"Yeah, she still loves him and everybody on the team knows not to go out with him. It's just not right."

"We found out yesterday that Melissa (a freshman) snuck out on a date with him last weekend. Now the whole team is choosing sides. I think it's just dumb. Who cares if she went out with him? He's gone out with, like, everybody."

"Still, we told Melissa it would be bad for the team, and she did it anyway. It's obvious she thinks her wants are more important than the team's needs."

It was pretty clear that the next day I wasn't going to be talking about how to turn excellent practice into a great performance as I had planned. Instead, I was going to be trying to sort out the drama of who was dating whose ex-boyfriend.

* * *

The *Stop The Drama!* campaign and this book were born out of my firsthand experience with teams caught up in the turmoil caused by gossip, back-stabbing, snubbing, and cliques—an all-too-common counterproductive cycle. As an athlete, I never understood why so much "nonsense" went on about things that had nothing to do with our becoming better athletes.

In high school, I remember thinking, "It will be so nice to get into the real world where people act like adults." Little did I know that adults engage in exactly the same drama as teenagers! I have watched drama stall and damage my recreational volleyball teams, my work groups, athletic teams I have consulted with, and coaches I have coached.

When I was able to go back to school and learn why drama happens, it was very clear: "Of course! It is a lack of effective communication." Looking at the skills provided to large corporations and high level executives, I thought, "I can teach those same skills to athletes!" So, I started building a framework that athletes, coaches, parents, and administrators can use to address the most common problems leading to miscommunication, conflict, and drama.

The stories you will find in this book are real. Some of them are directly from my life; some are from my experience consulting with teams and coaches; and some are from people who have shared their stories of the damage inflicted on them by drama. I have changed the names and some of the details to obscure the identities of those involved.

If you recognize yourself, your team, or your coach, it is likely because all teams become entangled in the same types of conflict, handle it in similar, unhealthy ways, and find themselves in a succession of downward spiraling arguments over "nothing."

You are not alone. Drama does happen, *but it doesn't have to.* The purpose of this book is to help you understand what is happening and *Stop The Drama!*

Do not feel like you have to read this book cover to cover before it will be helpful to you. Read Section One, which encompasses the first five chapters. They will provide you with a basic understanding of why drama happens and what you can do about it.

Section Two includes almost forty conversation-starter ideas, with each chapter centering on a single idea. Each subsection includes personal stories of drama and is written to stand on its own. They are short (about five pages each) and are designed to take no more than twenty minutes to read.

A team may decide to read the book together, assigning a subsection to be read and meeting to discuss it as a team. Or, an individual athlete, coach, parent, or administrator can read the book cover to cover to gain a better understanding of how teams communicate, why it is often unsuccessful, and what can be done about it. The choice is yours.

Section Three has tools many teams find useful as they strive toward better communication and productive conflict. You may also visit www.StopTheDramaNow.com and download printable copies of many of these tools.

At the end of each chapter, you will find a *My Communication Playbook* page like the one on the next page. Use it to write down points or page numbers that are particularly applicable to you and your team, exercises and tips you would like to implement, and things you'd like to share with others. It is your space to use as you see fit to create your Communication Game Plan to achieve even more from the potential of this book!

Use this book in the way that suits you and your team best. My wish for you is to have a drama-free season and it is my life's ambition to make a positive difference in as many lives as I can touch.

I ask you to help me by paying it forward. Share the skills you learn through this book and the *Stop The Drama!* campaign with others. Together, we will *Stop The Drama!* that is limiting our success!

MY COMMUNICATION PLAYBOOK

Section One

What is the deal with all the drama and what can we do about it?

Chapter One: Why Are Women So Catty?

The evolutionary, cultural, and learned reasons women are catty and use gossip, backstabbing, and cliques to address conflict. Additionally, why "Boys are easy; they just get into a fight and get over it. But girls hold a grudge for twenty years."

Chapter Two: Productive Conflict and Why it Works

Introduces productive conflict and explains how dealing with conflict in a healthy way keeps it from exploding later.

Chapter Three: Creating a Team Communication Fingerprint

Explains what a communication fingerprint is and introduces the idea of developing a team communication fingerprint.

Chapter Four: Creating a Plan for Success

A quick framework to team development that coaches and athletes can follow to get their team on the path towards less drama.

Chapter Five: Are You Planning to Fail?

Coaches and athletes sometimes think solving team drama is as simple as having a thirty minute conversation. This chapter explains that creating a new communication fingerprint takes time and effort just like learning a new pitch or a different style of defense.

Chapter One
Why Are Women So Catty?

A nation [a team] does not have to be cruel to be tough.

–Franklin Delano Roosevelt

Fear comes from not knowing how powerful you are.

–Unknown

It is awfully important to know what is, and what is not, your business.

–Gertrude Stein, "*What is English Literature*"

* * *

"I like your skirt. I have one just like it. Of course, mine is two sizes smaller."

"The reason the project failed is no one else worked as hard as I did."

"We lost the game because there isn't enough talent on this team. Sure, I'm a great player, but I can't always carry the whole game by myself."

"I saw your boyfriend talking to another woman this weekend. I guess he's just not that into you."

* * *

If you have worked with or been on an all-female team, doubtless you have seen this kind of behavior. If you have somehow managed to avoid it, look no further than reality TV—you will find countless examples of women using gossip, backstabbing, snubbing, cliques, and other drama in response to conflict.

So what is the deal? *Why do women behave that way?*

* * *

It seems to be a well-known "fact" that teams of male athletes get into fist fights and teams of female athletes have drama. *Tolerating* the damaging effects of drama as a cost of having female teams is preposterous. There are *reasons* why the cat fights, backstabbing, gossip, and cliques happen. The good news is there is a way to keep them from derailing *your* team.

What is Drama?

Female athletes are not the only people who use drama to address conflict. Tune into any reality show focusing on women and you will see drama—lots of it—often escalating into physical violence. Men even use drama when a physical altercation is out of the question. In the business world, it happens all the time—but, in that setting, it is known as "office politics."

Gossip is a big player in team drama. An athlete will broadcast details of a conflict to everyone except the person with whom they have a problem. The story will continue to be rehashed until it eventually gets back to the person in question.

Soon after, cliques start to form. Players, and even coaches, are pressured into taking sides. Someone will try to mediate the situation and become ostracized by *both* sides. Backstabbing becomes common place. Athletes, coaches, and parents who are not even involved with the team will jump into the emotional fray. This goes on and on for what seems like forever. I have worked with teams who were still fighting about something that happened four *years* ago!

With all the energy going into the 'battle', it is no wonder teams in the throes of emotional drama don't practice or compete up to their potential. Trying to coach a team in that condition is all but impossible. More than one coach has thought, "Just shut up and play!" Coaches feel out of control and frustrated. Outsiders (administration, parents, the front office) expect the coach to fix the problem, and think she is incompetent if she can't.

There is an unspoken expectation that becoming a coach makes one an expert in team communication and conflict, and that coaches should be able to keep drama from happening. Coaches are experts in *coaching* their sport, not team building or managing drama. Unresolved drama leads to dissatisfaction, burnout, and a strong dislike for coaching. More than one coach who had been passionate about their job has walked away from their sport because the drama was just too much for them.

Why Drama Happens

I am going to let you in on a secret: the use of drama by females and fighting by males as a way to handle conflict goes back as far as the dawn of humans. It isn't about poor coaching or bad athletes. When our ancestors where scrounging around for their next meal, fist fights made sense for men and ostracizing someone from the group was a reasonable way to get ahead for a woman.

Why Guys Have Fist Fights: Cavemen

Back several hundred millennia, a man's job was twofold: to kill something to eat and to protect his family from attack. To be successful, he needed to be physically strong and physically aggressive—you can't *talk* an animal to death no matter *how* hard you try. If our caveman friend got into an argument with another man, the best way to prove who was 'right' was for one of them to make the other incapable of fulfilling his hunter-protector role. That is best accomplished by inflicting physical injury.

Once it was established that one caveman was bigger and stronger than another, his way was deemed 'right' and the loser had no reason to engage the winner again and risk further injury. The argument was resolved until the loser believed he might have the upper hand and another physical altercation ensued. Basically, he who wins gets his way; he who loses shuts up and deals (unless he wants to get his backside kicked again).

Hence the belief that men fight and get it over with. But it is *not* actually over—it only *looks* resolved from the outside. The problem is really just buried until the loser thinks he could become the winner. I call this 'winner gets his way' method of dealing with conflict "King of the Jungle" or "Top Dog."

Why Women Use Drama: Cavewomen

Now consider the life of a cavewoman. She has several small children. She is responsible for gathering and cooking food, preparing and sewing hides to clothe her family, caring for the sick or injured, and doing everything else necessary to maintain her cave household.

All of those tasks could not be done alone. Cavewomen had to rely on each other for help: "You watch my kids and I'll gather enough berries for both of our families." This works great until there is a conflict.

For cavewomen, physically harming each other is counterproductive. An injured woman means two fewer hands available to get things done and having the added task of nursing her back to health. More work for the group—nobody needs that!

However, if Cavewoman Sally can convince the group that Cavewoman Jane is a bad person, the group will support Sally more and Jane less. Being able to remove someone from the group reduces the workload and increases resource availability (one less family to support).

Starting a rumor, talking behind Jane's back, and getting the group to choose Sally over Jane would accomplish getting Jane ousted from the group. "Did you hear what Cavewoman Jane did to my baby? Oh, it was *so* bad. I will never trust her with my children again!"

The problem: Jane is trying to convince the group that the exact opposite is true, and she isn't going to leave without a fight. She responds by trying to get the group on her side: "What I did wasn't so bad. Cavewoman Sally is the one you have to watch out for. I saw poisonous berries in her bucket yesterday. I wouldn't be surprised if her whole family gets sick!" See how cliques start to form? There is no way to choose a winner in that situation.

Pretty soon, the whole cave-complex is talking about Sally and Jane. Who is right and who is wrong? What actually happened and what is just a tall-tale made up by the gossip chain? It doesn't take long before even the men are involved: Sally and Jane both forbid their mates from speaking to each other.

And on it goes, until either Sally or Jane leaves the group—but even then, it might not be over. By that point there are so many other people involved that it doesn't end, it simply changes focus. Thus the creation of cliques, backstabbing, gossip, and drama, and the belief that women can hold grudges for twenty years!

The Psychology of Drama

When women attack relationships within a group, it is called *relational aggression*. Usually three groups develop: two sides and the middle. The people in the middle are trying to make things better or just ignore it. The people on each side try to get the people in the middle, and on the opposing side, to join them. With every circuit the drama grows.

When drama takes on a life of its own, I call it *firestorming* and there is no way for a coach or a leader to win. It is not usually the coach's *fault* (unless she or he is involved!), but it certainly is the coach's *problem*. No matter what choice is made, no one will be happy.

Inevitably, *everyone* ends up angry with the coach, and the problem escalates even further. Athletes feel like the coach isn't fixing the problem so they go over her or his head to the administration or the front office. I have seen more than one coach lose their job because of unresolved drama.

MY COMMUNICATION PLAYBOOK

Chapter Two
Productive Conflict and Why It Works

Anybody can become angry; that is easy; but to be angry with the right person, and to the right degree, and at the right time, and for the right purpose, and in the right way - that is not within everybody's power and is not easy.

–Aristotle

A false friend is more dangerous than an open enemy.

–Francis Bacon

* * *

The energy in the room was intense. The pressure of the hurt and the feelings of betrayal were so concentrated I could physically feel the anxiety. This was going to be a painful conversation for everyone—for the sisters who were also teammates as well as for me.

I had been working with the team once a week for only a few months, but I knew the older sister, Becky, had a serious crush on a boy named Jack. She talked about, emailed, Facebooked, and texted him. The couple of dates they had been on were so exciting she could barely contain herself.

So shock does not begin to describe how I felt when I picked up the phone and heard the coach say, "We have a problem. Ginny slept with Jack." *Really?!* Becky's younger sister and teammate had breached that type of trust? How was that possible? But that was the reality when I walked into the office. Becky sat in the corner sobbing while Ginny stood staring out the window. The coach brushed passed me to leave, and as the door closed he said, "Good luck." I took a deep breath.

"Ladies," I said simply. Ginny turned around. I noticed her makeup had been smeared and there were tears running down her face.

"I screwed up," was all she said. The torture she felt was apparent.

"How about you come and sit down with us so we can talk." I walked toward Becky and sat on the floor near her as Ginny joined us.

That is how a conversation filled with regret, anguish, and feelings of disloyalty started. After almost three hours of tears, anger, and frustration, there was an accepted apology and forgiveness. Their relationship as sisters would take time to heal, but as teammates they were able to move forward immediately.

A few years later I got an email from Becky thanking me for saving their relationship—it had been strained before Jack came onto the scene, and that incident was the culmination of what could have been a lifelong feud. Both Becky and Ginny strongly believed that my forcing them to talk it out in their coach's office made it something they could get over rather than a grudge they would hold onto forever.

* * *

The first thing you need to understand to make productive conflict work is that *not all conflict is bad*. If a team has no conflict at all, it means someone is lying, or at least hiding the truth. Great teams use productive conflict as a tool for creating good ideas and for becoming a better team. The second thing you need to understand is what productive conflict is and why it works.

What is Productive Conflict?

Productive conflict is realizing and creating an agreement between teammates that they will approach disagreement, misunderstanding, and differences of opinion using a standard set of guidelines. An additional part of the agreement is that firestorming will not be used and that issues will be taken directly to the person in question. (A team contract and a summary list of guidelines can be found in Section Three.)

At first, you might not think the words "productive" and "conflict" should go together. Conflict has a bad reputation as always being negative. The general feeling is that if people are disagreeing, it should be stopped. Years ago, I heard someone say, "If two or more people are working on something and there is no disagreement, someone is lying." What that means is that whether they say it out loud or not, people always have different ways of looking at the same situation.

Lack of discussion does not *mean agreement*. It just means someone doesn't want, or isn't allowed, to bring up a dissenting opinion. A situation like that creates a group of "yes-women" who will go along with anything rather than bring up a concern or a different idea.

That is not to say that all forms of conflict are good—quite the contrary. Drama is conflict and, obviously, it does really bad things to teams—screaming, spitting, and fist-fights in the locker room are bad for everybody, and are in no way productive. Let's look at a few ways I have seen players, coaches, and teams try to deal with disagreement and conflict, why they don't work, and how productive conflict is different.

Why Productive Conflict Works

At its core, productive conflict has the following characteristics:

Gives people a chance to tell their side of the story without the risk of being verbally or emotionally attacked;

Allows feelings to get out in the open rather than being bottled up and stewing;

Creates a safe space to work through misunderstandings;

Minimizes defensiveness and the winner/loser mentality;

Creates an environment where teammates can safely assume everyone involved is trying to achieve a positive result for the whole team;

Provides a framework for addressing conflict so it can be dealt with, addressed, and left behind rather than becoming an ongoing grudge match;

Provides a way for teammates or coaches to admit when they have made a mistake, apologize, and not be stigmatized for it.

The concept is pretty simple; the challenging part is getting your team to buy into it and use it. That is why setting a foundation for a team communication fingerprint is the first step. Becky and Ginny's team had created a team communication fingerprint prior to their incident, so we started from that agreed-upon point of trust in our difficult (but ultimately successful) conversation.

The next chapter will give you the groundwork to get your team on a path to creating a team communication fingerprint and being able to use productive conflict.

Methods That Don't Work

The Volcano—All of us have subscribed to this technique at some point. Something bothers us, but rather than say or do anything about it, we just push it down and ignore it, thinking it will go away. Over time, the pressure builds. Eventually something—possibly even just a 'small something'—will cause us to explode, spewing the hot lava of anger and frustration all over our unsuspecting teammates. One of the major issues with this method is the amount of time it takes to clean up. Not only does all the 'stuff' that was packed down for so long have to be addressed, so do the hurt feelings and damage done by the explosion. It is much messier than if each individual issue had been addressed at the time it occurred.

The Packrat—This is similar to the Volcano in that issues are being ignored; however, it is different because pressure *doesn't* build up and things *don't* usually explode. Instead, this person packs trunks of emotional stuff and stashes them all over their emotional space. No one, including the person herself, really knows when they might bump into one of those trunks and spill the contents. Doing so can lead to a variety of responses, from tears to screaming to sullenness or depression. As a result, members of the team will feel like they need to walk on eggshells around that person. Any issues or concerns that team members have will be ignored, because a disproportionate emotional response is always a risk.

The "Solver"—This person is all about getting issues out in the open, particularly ones that have nothing to do with her. She will gladly mediate conversations between teammates about their issues. Sharing 'concerns' about her teammates with others under the guise of being worried about them and wanting to be helpful is common. This person will always be 'in the know' about what is going on with whom. If you need the latest juicy gossip, she is the go-to person. The reality of a

Solver is that she actually isn't solving anything—she is simply stirring the pot and fanning the flames of a firestorm. Additionally, it is likely she is hiding concerns and issues about herself behind all the noise of trying to 'help' everyone else.

Pollyanna - Nothing is ever wrong here. The world is all sunshine and rainbows; no worries at all. A team member who always looks at the world through rose-colored glasses will quickly find herself discounted and even ostracized by her teammates. Even when she has good ideas, they will be ignored. Coaches tend to love players like this because they are easy to work with. Making them a coach's pet will only deepen the gulf between them and their teammates. Being positive is great, as long as the person is willing to listen and try to understand team concerns.

Toxic Churn—The opposite of Pollyanna, this person believes things are horrible and getting worse. Poking old wounds is a specialty. Conflict is never over. Grudges are a given. As an old country song puts it, "bury the hatchet, but leave the handle sticking out." Firestorming is great fun and complaining is the norm. You can read more about how to deal with toxic people in Chapter Eight.

The Terminator—This method is found most often in coaches and athletic administration. They try to take the easy way out of conflict. They fire, cut, penalize, remove from the game, and otherwise punish anyone who doesn't do things their way. This method creates a scared team of yes-women. They won't play brave and give everything they've got, because they will be too scared of making a mistake. Such a coach might get a winning game, maybe even a winning season, but top talent will not be able to maintain performance at and above their potential if they are always afraid the rug will be pulled out from under them.

When I speak to coaches, athletes, and parents about the various unhealthy methods people use to deal with differences or conflict, there is always laughter. I bet as you read through them you were able to think of at least a couple of people you know who use these strategies; maybe you even recognized yourself in some of them. Now that you know how to recognize several methods that *don't* work, let's talk about the one that *does*.

MY COMMUNICATION PLAYBOOK

Chapter Three
Creating a Team Communication Fingerprint

Any (wo)man worth (her) salt will stick up for what (s)he believes is right, but it takes a slightly better (wo)man to acknowledge instantly and without reservation that (s)he is in error.

–Andrew Jackson

The trouble with most of us is that we would rather be ruined by praise than saved by criticism.

–Norman Vincent Peale

* * *

"I was *not* rude!"

"If you are so clueless as to think *that* is being respectful, I *refuse* to even *talk* to you!"

"I can't believe you are so thin-skinned. I was *just* kidding, *jeez*."

The exchange ended as one girl stomped away and the other shrugged and rolled her eyes. I knew it wasn't over, but just on hold until the next time they crossed paths—and it wasn't going to be pretty.

* * *

It has been said that one of the things which separates humans from animals is our ability to communicate with one another. I don't know about that—I've watched bees, ants, and flocks of birds that seem to communicate better than a lot of humans. Maybe that is because we are trying to communicate abstract ideas and feelings using concrete language. If we took the time to build some structure around what the words mean on an interpersonal level, we would have a better foundation for healthy, productive communication.

My brother is a mechanical engineer. He recently shared this frustrating conversation he had with a company salesman:

Brother: "You told the customer we could do this. How does this part of the machine work?"

Salesman: "I don't know. I hoped you could figure it out."

Brother: "Well, I can always put in a black box and just hope for a miracle."

Many people approach communication that way. They say, "I am an excellent communicator. I always say exactly what I mean. I can't help it if other people don't understand." That is like putting thoughts and ideas in the black box of hope and expecting perfect results. This is the picture of what that looks like:

It doesn't matter how fluent you believe you are or how well you think you are explaining something; if the person you are talking to hears a different message than you intended, the communication failed. Fortunately, there are ways to reduce the risk of miscommunication—it just takes a little bit of conversation maintenance.

Individual Communication Fingerprint

We learn to communicate from the people around us. As children, we learn from our parents, our teachers, and our friends. We start to understand how the meaning of a word can be altered by inflection and context. What is funny, rude, or sarcastic becomes clearer. Each interaction hones our skill in understanding the 95% of communication that is based on tone, body language, or facial expression and has nothing to do with the actual words spoken.

* * *

When I was a preteen, I was making myself a sandwich at the kitchen table when my four-year-old brother asked who the sandwich was for. I responded, rather sarcastically, "yours truly." I thought I had clearly communicated that I was making it for myself, however, when I took the first bite, he started to cry, claiming that I was eating *his* sandwich.

I explained to Dad that I had said the sandwich was for me. Dad pointed out that a four-year-old did not understand that "yours truly" meant me. I had to hand over the sandwich to my brother and make myself another one. I learned that I needed to be more straightforward when speaking to my younger siblings (and to make more than one sandwich at a time).

A few years later, I was visiting my aunt and was told to make myself a sandwich. I laid out enough bread for everyone in the room and started asking what everyone wanted. My aunt and uncle laughed at me because to me "make yourself a sandwich" meant "make sandwiches for everyone." The communication fingerprint I had learned at home did not translate to my aunt's house.

* * *

Since each of our lives is unique, everyone develops a distinctive, ingrained style of communication—their individual communication fingerprint. People from the same family tend to communicate in a similar fashion. Individuals from the same region of the country communicate in a similar style, and people from the same country are likely to understand each other better than those from another country, even if they speak the same language. On a team of only ten people, there are likely to be ten distinctly different styles and expectations of communication.

The more diverse the experiences on the team are, the greater the difference in their communication fingerprints will be, and the greater their risk of miscommunication. No wonder we often struggle to get our points across to one another!

Team Communication Fingerprint

If a team of people working together is going to be successful, they must develop a *team communication fingerprint.* Many teams create their communication style by putting things through the Black Box of Hope. Adjustments are made by backtracking when miscommunications, misunderstandings, hurt feelings, resentment, or anger get in the way of progress. These teams repeat the same painful process every time someone new arrives.

A better option is to take the proactive approach: figure out how to have successful communication right from the start. Create a way to explain how things work to new team members so they can get up to speed very quickly. It is unfortunate how many teams choose the Black Box of Hope.

Developing a team communication fingerprint takes deliberate, thoughtful action. Without planning, the default method is drama.

Coaching staff and athletes need to be willing to adjust their thinking and work on adapting their communication style into something that works toward the betterment of the team. The point is to get everyone—coaches and athletes alike—on the same communication frequency. If there is a discussed and accepted strategy for handling disagreement and conflict, the members of the team will hold each other accountable to not using drama and will be able to solve many of their internal squabbles without involving the coach or the administration.

A robust fingerprint will create an emotionally safe environment where mistakes are accepted as part of the learning process—where the question "how can I help you" is heard more often than "why did you do that?" Athletes will learn to play brave, knowing that, if they stretch a little too far, their teammates will be there to catch them. It is impossible to know the true potential of a team if they are afraid to make mistakes. And they will be afraid to make mistakes if there is a constant fear they will be judged or punished rather than coached and helped.

That all sounds great. But how-in-the-world do you get your team to have a communication fingerprint that works for everyone? That is the point of this book! With some time and effort, I know your team can be well on its way to creating a communication fingerprint for themselves.

Building the Foundation for Communication

Sit down as a team and get buy-in from everyone. Have everyone talk about what it means to them to be part of the program; what they think it takes to be an elite athlete; their passion for the sport; their commitment to doing everything in their power—physically, mentally, and emotionally—to make the most of their potential and to do their part to create the most competitive team possible. Coaches should feel free to join in the discussion and share their enthusiasm, too! This may seem like a given. But, too often, athletes feel like they are the only person on the team who is truly committed to success. When they hear excitement and zeal for the game from their teammates, it will build on itself. In addition to creating a team passion, the conversation will build trust and the secure feeling that everyone is committed and no one wants to let the team down.

Learn about each individual communication fingerprint. Ask questions about communication style. Go around the room and let everyone answer. This exercise also builds team trust, because they will be getting to know each other. Some example questions:

If someone hurts your feelings, are you more likely to confront them or just let it slide? Why?

On teams you've been on before, when you felt like one of your teammates was slacking off during practice, what did you do? Why?

When you are overwhelmed or stressed, what do you do? What can your teammates look for to know you are stressed and might need some support?

What types of things make you feel the most supported? This one might take a little encouragement. I have had success by asking athletes to think about their "go-to" person—when the chips are down and they really need somebody, who do they turn to? What does that person do for them? Answers I have heard vary: "Just let me vent," "Problem solved with me," and "Told me what to do" are some common answers.

If someone has a problem with you or wants to give you feedback, how do you like to hear it?

What do you think when a teammate cries? I have found this question brings up a lot about expectations, toughness, acceptance, and which emotions are "okay" emotions versus which are not. Coaches (particularly male coaches) should be careful not to influence the conversation. Tears are simply the expression of emotion, like laughing, and should not be stifled. However, tears used for manipulation are completely unacceptable.

Discuss as a team how disagreements, feedback, and conflict should be handled. *The Seven No-Fail Secrets to Stop The Drama!* and *The Nine Secrets to Great Teamwork* are great places to start. (See Section Three.)

Create a team contract, either verbal or written (see Section Three for a sample contract). I have seen teams include it in their Code of Conduct or make it big enough to hang on a locker room wall for all to sign. Do what works best for your team.

A healthy team communication fingerprint requires ongoing conversations. Each of the upcoming chapters will help coaches and athletes learn more about themselves and each other. The better you understand each other, what is needed, and how to provide it, the more smoothly your team will function. It will become easy to focus on the technical and physical skills needed to get the highest level performance from your team, because issues and problems will be addressed and forgotten!

MY COMMUNICATION PLAYBOOK

Chapter Four
Creating a Plan for Success

A bad habit never disappears miraculously; it's an undo-it-yourself project.
–Abigail Van Buren

All glory comes from daring to begin.
–Eugene F. Ware

Don't live down to expectations. Go out there and do something remarkable.
–Wendy Wasserstein

If you judge a fish by his ability to climb a tree he will spend his entire life believing he is stupid.
–Albert Einstein

* * *

You've decided you want things to be better on your team. You want to be able to communicate the things that need to be communicated quickly and easily while minimizing the risk of misunderstanding and hurt feelings. You want conflict to be addressed and resolved before it becomes a huge firestorm. In short, you want the drama to stop so you can focus on coaching, playing, improving, and winning!

Wonderful! You have made the first step toward making things better: you know there is a problem and you want to fix it. But now what? It's not like there is a manual that will tell you how to *Stop The Drama*! Well, actually, you are in luck—there *is* such a manual, and you are holding it! So let's get right into it.

The Plan of Attack

First and foremost, you have to realize this is a major undertaking that must be done in small steps. You are trying to change your team's dynamics—the very foundation of how they interact with each other. It will make them better as individuals and as a team both on and off the field. They will have more time and energy to use toward being an athlete, and you will see better performances, potential met and exceeded, and happier athletes. But you *must* commit to putting in the time and the effort.

If you think you can give it lip service by telling your team they 'should' change, 'need' to change, or simply demand that they change, and believe that is going to be enough to actually create change, you might as well put this book down right now. It takes about eight weeks of consistent effort to address existing issues and start to see a change in how your team communicates. It will take at least a full season of working together before they are good at it. And then, if you are like most teams, your most senior players (who picked up the skills the fastest and the best) will leave and you will get a whole group of newbies who know nothing of your team's methods. Don't worry—I'll show you how to deal with that. For now, realize you are committing to a long-term project that is going to make a huge positive difference on your team.

Don't be discouraged. The rewards of a team with a healthy communication fingerprint are huge! Here are just a few words I have heard from coaches and athletes to describe their teams who have implemented *Stop The Drama!*: "smooth," "easy," "fun," "comfortable," "It just clicks," "We get each other," "Best team I have ever been on and worked with," "We win!", "We know how to learn from mistakes," "No more stupid fights." Does that sound like a team *you* would like to be on? You *can* be! You have the power to make it happen.

Who is Involved?

Who is the focus of this project? Every team is made up of groups of smaller teams. Generally, there are three possible groups: the athletes, the coaching staff, or the athletes and coaching staff combined. Sometimes large teams have sub-teams (offense and defense for example). How your communication plan is designed and implemented will depend on which of those groups is the focus. The programs which are most successful consider the athletes and the coaching staff separately, but create communication plans for both groups which use a similar communication fingerprint. Focusing exclusively on the athletes can create a situation where the athletes' communication and conflict skills improve and they become frustrated that the coaching staff is still using old methods.

While it is possible to create a professional development program for only the coaching staff, and even a single coach, this book focuses on the whole team. If you decide to create a communication fingerprint for just your athletes, be careful not to point at them as being the only source of the problem. Make sure you learn along with them. After all, whatever skills (or lack thereof) you use they will follow, regardless of what they are being taught.

What Do You Need?

Let's assume that we are focusing on the athletes on your team. That means *all* the athletes: injured players, red-shirting players, offense *and* defense, swimmers *and* divers, everybody. If you decide not to include everybody, you are creating separate and distinct teams and they will view themselves that way. If you want them to behave like a single unit, treat them as one.

Any team of young women that has been in existence for more than a minute has past issues. Some are big; some are small; some involve current players; and sometimes the issues are leftover 'stuff' from athletes long moved on. Whatever it is—no matter how ridiculous it seems—you have to get it out on the table. I have had good success with giving everybody a couple of index cards and asking questions like:

What does a great team look like?

What does it feel like to be on a healthy, high functioning team?

What does this team need to become healthy and high functioning?

What topics does our team need to talk about?

What about this team causes you stress?

If you are the coach, you might run into a little resistance to this exercise. Players may worry that you will recognize their handwriting and use their answers against them. The best way to keep this from being an issue is to bring someone in from the outside to help you. If that is not an option, do everything in your power to reassure your athletes that it is not your intention to set them up to be punished.

You have one shot at gaining their trust—if you blow it, you will not get another one. Additionally, if your athletes have concerns about you or other members of your staff, you are unlikely to learn about it the first time you ask. However, if you create a successful program and your athletes honestly believe you are trying to produce the healthiest, highest-functioning, best-performing team possible, they will eventually feel safe enough to provide feedback about you.

Gather All the Information

Consider asking your coaching staff the same questions to see what they think, then dig into it. Type it up, sort the cards into piles, color them with highlighters, or make notes on them—whatever works for you. Figure out what your team needs to discuss in order to make the past the past. I know what you are thinking, "I don't know anything about analyzing this type of stuff." I know, I hear you. But unless you have a budget to hire someone or are fortunate enough to have a psychology department with graduate students looking for an internship, you are their only hope. Trust me, it will be worth it.

Create Ground Rules

There are lots of ideas and specifics in the remainder of this book about how to create and enforce communication ground rules. I certainly recommend reading all of it before you decide to pull your team into a room and talk about whatever issues they wrote on the cards. You are going into an emotionally charged situation with emotionally charged subjects. There will be tears—possibly lots of them. I have been in meetings where the whole team was crying by the end.

If you aren't prepared to manage this, you may not only *not* help your team, you may make the situation *worse*. Opening a can of worms is only productive when each 'worm' is addressed and resolved. Leave a 'worm' out to fester, and your team is likely to end up firestorming about it. Picking worms up and putting them back in the can makes everyone feel jerked around and emotionally raw for no reason. So pick your 'worms' wisely. If you absolutely feel like you can't wait until you have finished the book to implement these ideas, at least look at *The Seven No-Fail Secrets to Stop The Drama!* and *The Nine Secrets to Great Teamwork* in Section Three—they will give you a place to start.

Get Buy-in

It is important that the team believes this process is going to be helpful and worth their time. If they are in a lot of emotional pain—committed to doing anything within the law to get an edge over their opponents, or they believe their opponents already have the leg up because they have a program like this—you are in luck. Keep in mind they don't all have to be onboard on Day One. They can be skeptical as long as they are willing to give it a try.

Once you have 30% of the emotional power on the team on board, the rest will come along and even join in. Try not to tell them they "have" to do this. Instead, explain how it will benefit them.

If you are fortunate enough to have emotionally mature athletes—even just a few—they will be a great help. Suggest everyone read this book to get them thinking on the same page. Parents who are influential can be involved if that works for your team. Invite other coaches to engage in a friendly communication fingerprint development challenge. Maybe your administration is particularly connected to your team—ask them to become supporters. Anything you can do to make this the "in" thing to do, do it. Your athletes will thank you; not only because it will make the team better, but because they will be able to use the communication skills they learn now for the rest of their lives.

Make Time!

The next chapter is all about making time and why it is important, so I won't go into it here. Simply put: you can only expect to get *out* in proportion to what you put *in*. There will be no change without practice, and there will be no practice without scheduling time.

Pull the Trigger

Once you have all the pieces in place and you feel like you are prepared to facilitate a few of these meetings (or have someone facilitate for you), go for it! Just don't forget the next step:

Ask for Feedback

No program works flawlessly. Be willing to make adjustments as you go. Don't make changes in a vacuum based on what you think is or isn't working. *Ask!* This is a *team* program and *team* communication fingerprint—everyone has to be involved in making it work.

Give out more index cards. Ask them what they like, don't like, and how things are going. Over time, you won't need the index cards. They will start to trust you and each other and feel safe enough to just talk about how things are going. In the beginning, if you want truthful answers, you are better off giving them the option of being anonymous.

Celebrate!

You will know when you have it: the elusive "it" of a team that works. There will be no drama. Minor issues or hiccups will be addressed and resolved. Don't forget to talk about how great it is, and how you want to keep it going!

MY COMMUNICATION PLAYBOOK

Chapter Five
Are You Planning to Fail?

Don't say you don't have enough time. You have exactly the same number of hours per day that were given to Helen Keller, Pasteur, Michelangelo, Mother Teresa, Leonardo da Vinci, Thomas Jefferson, and Albert Einstein.

–H. Jackson Brown, Jr.

Everything looks impossible for the people who never try anything.

–Jean-Louis Etienne

Nothing worth gaining is ever without effort.

–Theodore Roosevelt

* * *

Would you expect a pitcher to be able to throw a new pitch after listening to the coach describe the mechanics of it? How about expecting a swimmer to change her stroke in competition based on reading an article? A gymnast to execute a new routine flawlessly because she saw a video of someone *else* doing it? Or for your team to implement a new defense or attack based only on the X's and O's on a whiteboard? Clearly you wouldn't. There would be practice, practice, and more practice. You would watch, critique, assess, analyze, and bring in experts. Work would be done for days, months, even seasons, to perfect the change.

So why is it that we, as athletes, believe something as engrained as how we communicate can be changed any other way? We, better than anyone else, understand the need for practice. Of course, reading a book is a great place to start. I hope this book becomes dog-eared and highlighted with comments written in the margins and on sticky notes stuck on every page. I hope you get a copy for each team member to build a foundation for healthy team communication.

But a book (even this book) is not enough by itself. Communication has to be *practiced*—and not just halfhearted when-we-feel-like-it practice. I am talking about all-out, leave-your-heart-on-the-field, give-everything-you've-got-and-then-give-some-more practice. And that only happens when time is scheduled to *make* it happen.

* * *

No Pain, No Gain?

How much pain is your team experiencing due to poor communication? How much energy is being wasted on gossip and drama? How much of your potential are you giving away to conflict before you so much as step foot in a competition? How many W's are you giving away because your team doesn't talk and understand each other on the field?

If you haven't been willing to make time to learn how to have healthy communication and productive conflict, then the answer to those questions is "not enough." Maybe you are one of those people who must hit rock bottom and start digging before you can even think about solving a problem. Maybe you think things aren't "so bad" with your team. Maybe you think they should just "shut up and play." Since you are reading this book, I doubt this is true. In fact, I bet the opposite. You are looking for an edge so your team can be even more successful. If so, you have come to the right place!

* * *

I know of a coach who waited to ask for help until half her team was involved in a wet t-shirt competition at a local bar. Several of the girls were underage, most had been drinking, and all were wearing team t-shirts with the school logo on them. Imagine the conversation when a member of the community called just to "let the coach know." The coach was mortified. Why didn't anyone on that team speak up? Why didn't someone say, "hey, this is a bad idea"?

It isn't because nobody thought it. Several players admitted—after the fact—they knew a wet t-shirt contest of any kind was a bad idea and more so in team t-shirts. The reason they gave for not saying anything? *They didn't know how.* They had no way to confront their teammates. They were afraid they would be seen as a "wet-blanket" and that they would be laughed at and ignored.

* * *

Be Proactive—Starting Right Now

How bad do things have to get, how much potentially permanent emotional damage has to be done before you will begin to build a foundation for your athletes to be able to speak up when they know something is wrong? I hope you didn't pick up this book because your team is in that place; I hope you are being *pro*active. Either way, now is the right time to start your team on the path to healthy communication and productive conflict.

It all starts with scheduling regular team meetings to learn and practice new, healthy communication skills. I recommend an hour a week. If you simply can't see any way to make that happen, then shoot for every other week. Maybe the best you can do is a seminar or a speaker or two. Okay, do that, but make sure it is interactive with ideas for behavioral change, not just somebody speaking *at* your team about the importance of communication. Remember, your athletes will only value the process as much as you do. You can only expect to get positive outcome in proportion to the positive you put into the process.

To start, follow the ideas in the previous chapters. Don't forget to discuss *The Seven No-Fail Secrets to Stop The Drama!* and *The Nine Secrets to Great Teamwork* (found in Section Three). Once you have a communication fingerprint in place and a contract to follow, pick a topic in this book or a communication idea you found somewhere else and open a discussion about it.

Take *The Golden Rule is Failing Us* (Chapter Seven) as an example:

What do your players think about that?

Do they agree? Disagree? Why?

What examples do they have about how they (personally) like to be treated?

What does respect mean to them?

How could they recognize when someone is applying the Golden Rule but it's not the way they want to be treated?

What words could they use to gain that kind of knowledge from each other?

What do they need from each other to feel supported?

Give Everyone a Chance to Speak

In itself, the process of having the discussion will teach your team a lot about each other. Observe who speaks up and who doesn't. Do the dominant personalities talk over or ignore the more passive ones? Ask them about it. What do they think should be done? Do they even realize it is happening? How does it feel?

Trust me, a discussion like this can get really lively. Make sure that everyone who wants to speak has a chance to feel heard. Feeling heard is important. (See Chapter Seven for more on making someone feel heard.)

When players feel like their comments are being glossed over or ignored, they will shut down and stop sharing. Check in with players who aren't speaking. Maybe they have something to share that is being lost. Then again, maybe they don't, but *check*.

Make sure you, or someone the team respects, will be facilitating the meeting. Attacking, name calling, and personal insults should not be tolerated. Using *The Seven No-Fail Secrets to Stop The Drama!* and *The Nine Secrets to Great Teamwork* will keep the meeting from deteriorating into a spiral of complaints and anger which will make things worse, not better. Tears are okay; hurting each other is not.

At the end of the meeting—and you are likely to have to call an end because teams can get really into these types of discussions—ask your team what it was like to participate in this exercise. Weird? Fun? Interesting? Different? What did they learn about the topic or each other? What could you do differently next time to make it better?

If you are the one running the meetings, don't judge; *listen, listen, listen*. And certainly don't tell someone they are wrong. This is the team's time to grow. Of course, that doesn't mean the coaching staff can't do exactly the same thing—you are a team, too. You can benefit just as much as they can from healthy communication and productive conflict!

You are Limited Only by Your Imagination

If you run out of topics from this book, or want to talk about something more personal, ask your team about other conflicts they are having at the moment or have had in the past that they would like to discuss. Brainstorm ideas for solving an issue in a productive way. Maybe there is an issue with another team that needs to be addressed. Maybe someone has a problem with a parent, professor, or friend with which they would like help. It is even likely there is an issue within your team that they want to talk about or work out.

I worked with a team that would email me topics throughout the week and then if no one brought up anything pressing at our next meeting, we would pick a topic out of the hat and discuss it. The possibilities are endless. With some creativity from you or your facilitator and a team who is willing to learn, successful communication is yours for the taking. It is really as simple as making the time and practicing.

MY COMMUNICATION PLAYBOOK

Section Two

Many of the things teams leave up to chance. Quick reads on topics teams struggle with, tips, tricks and ideas on how to get teams talking and ways to create healthy, cohesive, productive teams who get more from their existing potential.

Chapter Six: Creating the Framework for Great Teamwork

Create the foundation you need to build a successful team communication fingerprint, engage in effective communication, and use productive conflict.

Chapter Seven: Communication is the Heart of Success

Challenge your assumptions about how communication works; the ground floor of any successful communication fingerprint.

Chapter Eight: Productive Conflict will Save You

Build on your understanding of communication by learning to deal with disagreements and conflict; key to teams and individuals who want to function at their peak.

Chapter Nine: Be a Great Leader

Take the skills you have learned, build an amazing team and lead them to success. Being a leader is more than being a manager.

Chapter Ten: Get More from Your Potential

It isn't only about how you communicate with others—learn to communicate with yourself to achieve your highest potential.

Chapter Eleven: Bonus Topics

A couple of topics too important to leave out.

Chapter Six
Creating the Foundation for Great Teamwork

Talent wins games, but teamwork and intelligence win championships.

–Michael Jordan

Let go of your attachment to being right, and suddenly your mind is more open. You're able to benefit from the unique viewpoints of others, without being crippled by your own judgment.

–Ralph Marston

If my aim is to prove I am "enough" the project goes on to infinity because the battle was already lost on the day I conceded the issue was debatable.

–Nathaniel Branden

* * *

The 411 on Productive Conflict

Danielle stormed into the locker room. "Where is she? Where is that %$#@?!?!

The team looked at each other. They were sure she was talking about Lacey. "Don't know. We haven't seen her yet," someone ventured.

Lacey's timing couldn't have been worse as she walked through the door. Danielle spun around, eyes blazing. "You stupid, two-faced, lying pig!" she screamed. "Did you really think you could hide it? That I wouldn't find out?"

Lacey went from dumbfounded to attack mode instantly. "Me? *You're* the hypocrite!"

They stood, faces inches apart, screaming and cursing at each other. After Danielle spit in Lacey's face, they had to be pulled apart and restrained. It was *not* a good day to be on that team.

* * *

Types of conflict

Conflict comes in two forms: *how* you argue and *what* you argue about can improve or deteriorate what you get from your potential. It's true that disagreements like the one above are obviously damaging to the team and the individuals involved, however, it is possible to have even heated discussions in a way that creates resolution rather than more strife. The key is to recognize the type of conflict you are having and turn it into something that works to the advantage of everyone.

Relationship conflict

Try not to get too caught up in the term "relationship." In this context, we are not talking about a romantic relationship. Instead, the term is used to mean interpersonal interaction between two people—relationship conflict revolves around who someone *is* as a person. Arguments will include words meant to tear down or damage the other person's character: "stupid", "dumb", "doesn't think", "cares only about herself", "isn't interested in the good of the team", "backstabbing", or other nasty opinions. These character judgments may include examples to "prove" that what is being said is true. Additionally, relationship conflict involves trying to get the team to believe the other person is bad and you are good. The cavewomen in Chapter One were using relationship conflict, and so are Danielle and Lacey.

Here in the twenty-first century, relationship conflict accomplishes absolutely nothing—unless you think hurt feelings, grudges, and cliques are something worth striving for. It creates a defensive response, hurt feelings, and resentment. There is no upside to these types of arguments. There is no way for anyone to win—everyone will lose. Even worse, relationship conflict masks the real problem—such as unmet expectations or feelings of betrayal—burying it to fight another day. A *lose-lose situation.* Team and individual performance will suffer on and off the field, and a coach will spend time and energy having to mediate when a team is involved in relationship conflict.

Cognitive conflict

In contrast, cognitive conflicts (also called *informational differences*), are about the actual topics and issues at hand. The conversation might be about how something is or is not being accomplished, a situation that took place, how it was perceived by the people involved and the feelings that resulted, or any other number of real things.

Cognitive conflict is productive. You will not hear accusations about someone's character or declarations as to why someone else is behaving in a certain way. Disagreements of this type involve the *sharing of information*. There are lots of "I" statements: "I felt this way", "I observed this behavior", "I had this reaction." They do not include outside parties who are not a part of the problem being discussed. People who are working through a difference in opinion about their thoughts, feelings, and perceptions about a specific situation do not need to bring in other people, because they are working through what is going on in their head, not what other people think about it.

Informational differences move people towards resolution. As information about the real problem is shared, understanding grows and *win-win solutions* can be discovered. Cognitive conflict improves performance in both physical and mental activities.

Why conflict happens

Why do women create a firestorm of emotional drama rather than just deal with the person directly in a productive manner? Why do we draw in and spew out everyone within emotional miles? The simple answer: girls are taught to be 'nice' and we hate conflict. We pretend all is well while venting our frustration to anyone who will listen, gathering emotional support and ammunition for the clash we know is coming. When we do finally confront someone, it is a full attack with all guns blazing. It is not at all productive—in fact, it is devastating to the team as well as to all the individuals involved.

How to fix it

Rather than letting conflict build until it is out of control, address it right away. Create a team agreed-upon plan for addressing and resolving issues and problems as they come up. Commit to addressing concerns when they are small and manageable, directly with the person(s) involved and no one else. Once agreement has been reached, everyone (coaches and athletes alike) is responsible for holding each other accountable to stick to it.

A healthy team will not tolerate gossip and screaming as acceptable forms of communication. Drama feeds off the swirling emotions of a story being told over and over until it is whipped into a frenzy. It is amazing how quickly it all dies out when no one is there to listen and two people sit down to talk through it.

Sounds pretty easy, right? Ban all gossip and screaming and the drama will stop. Sorry, it is *not* that easy. It takes a plan, practice, hard work, commitment, and time.

I am assuming here you have already created a team communication fingerprint; see Chapter Three if you have not. This is the process for using your team's communication fingerprint for productive conflict:

Have each person share/explain her side of the story. Use *The Seven No-Fail Secrets to Stop The Drama!*

Listen so you can understand the whole story. Use active listening and self-awareness. The facilitator is responsible for pointing out the different issues within the main problem. Often hurt feelings and misunderstandings compound an issue and need to be untangled from other concerns. In some cases, the discussion process might be all you need. Understanding the other person's thoughts and feelings about a situation may be enough to elicit an apology for the misunderstanding and the ability to move past it. If that is not the case, continue the process.

Brainstorm solutions. What options are available to solve the issue? Remember: don't judge solutions as good or bad, just put them on the table.

Discuss the pros and cons of the available solutions.

Agree on a solution as a team or involved individuals.

Assign action items as needed.

Execute the plan.

Evaluate the result. Take time to get together to talk about the issue again a week or so later to make sure it has been resolved and does not need to be addressed any further. If it is not resolved, repeat the above process to understand what is missing. Discuss why the previous solution didn't work. However, if everyone concurs the problem is resolved, agree that it is over-and-done with and will not be brought up again.

If anyone tries to bring up the problem again or use it as evidence against someone, they should be reminded that the issue is in the past, is resolved, and that they agreed it was over.

When to Bring in Outside Help

Sometimes athletes are unwilling to talk about the concerns they have with each other when the coaching staff is in the room. They may worry that they will be judged negatively and punished for having "petty" problems. It can be even tougher if the problem they are having is with the coach. How do they begin to learn to deal with issues head-on if they are afraid to take the first step and talk about them?

If you find yourself in a situation where the team is saying that everything is fine but it clearly is not, a trusted, outside facilitator is your best bet. The person you need must be good at managing group discussion. Knowing when to let a conversation go on in order to get the problem out in the open, when to protect someone from a personal attack, and how to coax out the truth in a safe, productive manner are all key qualities. In addition, the coaching staff must have unequivocal faith that the person will have their back with the team. Never, ever, ever should a facilitator take sides or play middleman (See Section Three for more information about what to look for in a good communication program).

Confidentiality is of the utmost importance (read more about confidentiality later in this chapter). A team should never be allowed to destroy the coach's character. Coaches are not always right but they *are* always the coach. It is a fine line that allows the team to work through an issue without it becoming a gripe-moan-and-trash-each-other-or-the-coach session.

Problems should be discussed one at a time and in enough depth to get the whole story on the table. A good facilitator will know when to stop the rehashing of what happened and start problem solving. More times than I can count, I have said something like "Okay, let me make sure I understand what took place..." I summarized what I heard, asked if I had missed any of the major details, and then asked, "Where do we go from here?" "What would make the situation better?" "What do you need to move past this?" Talking about a problem is often cathartic. Coming up with a solution is liberating, empowering, and productive.

Who is involved and who is simply affected?

Issues that involve the whole team should be discussed with the whole team present. I know it is hard to get everyone together, but trust me, it is vital and worth it. If someone is missing when a problem is discussed and resolved, she will feel left out and may become ostracized from the group if she doesn't agree with the solution. Or, worse, if she has power in the group, she may reopen a closed issue and the whole conflict can start again.

Only those members involved in the conflict should be present when working through the issue. I have had meetings with five members of a team, who also were roommates, to address a conflict that had nothing to do with their sport but was affecting their ability to practice and play together. I have also met with as few as two athletes to help them work through an issue. Bring in everyone involved, but people who are not involved do not need to be there.

Issues involving the coach are a little trickier. In every case when I have worked with a team, concerns about the coach have been brought up. How they were handled varied from situation to situation and team to team. I always make it very clear to everyone from the start that I am *not* a middleman. I do not take information from the team meeting to the coach or from the coach to the team. If they have a problem with each other they need to talk about it—and most often that responsibility falls to the team captains. In some cases, I have facilitated discussion between captains and coaches, or been asked to sit in on meetings between coaches and individual players. This works only when the players and coaching staff have absolute trust that I am fair and will not choose sides.

In one instance, I was involved in a case where the entire team believed there was a problem they needed to bring to the coach's attention but everyone, even the captains, believed the coach would retaliate. In that case, since no one was willing to speak to the coach, we set up a way for them to give anonymous feedback via a box in the locker room. Unfortunately, it turned out the athletes were correct: the coach was unwilling to accept feedback from his athletes and refused to read their concerns. It was an unfortunate decision. The players were not heard by their coach, and they voiced those feelings very strongly to the administration. That coach's contract was not renewed the following year.

In a case where I have worked directly with a coach on "executive coaching for coaches," I have asked the team's permission to discuss broad, general topics of concern with the coach. This scenario is only an option when I have been involved in team development with the entire team in conjunction with professional development for the coach. And I have been fortunate to have had very positive results in this dual role. However, I cannot overstate how critical it was to have had absolute transparency between myself and the players and between myself and the coach. The lines of confidentiality were drawn very clearly, and I had regular conversations about how and what information was (or was not) to be shared. I would not recommend this role for the untrained facilitator.

Finding a qualified facilitator

I bet you are thinking to yourself, "Great, how am I going to find a talented, trained, ethical, unbiased facilitator?" If you are lucky to have administration who understands the need for a professional, and you have money in your budget, double bonus for you. Look in the community for facilitators trained in team building/team development. If you want professional development for yourself or your staff, look for an executive coach who has an athletic background. There are not many who specifically cross over into the athletic world, but the skills they teach to executives will be beneficial to you, too.

Keep looking until you find one who understands you are an executive in your own right and who is willing to work with you. Individuals with a psychology or counseling background are a good place to start for both team and professional development.

In my experience, the unfortunate reality is that most program leaders do not see the value in team or professional development, and will cut a coach's attempt to put funding in the budget for it. If you are in that situation, not all is lost. If you are affiliated with a university, check with the counseling program. Even if you are not, look into psychology or counseling graduate programs. Very often there are advanced students looking for practice hours who might be willing and able to help you. Additionally, you might be able to find someone in your community who is willing to work with your team pro bono.

Regardless of whom you bring in, take the time to interview them just like you would a potential player or a new member of your coaching staff. You need a personality that fits with your team and someone everyone can trust. Find the right person and the benefits will be amazing! Once you and your team trust each other to use *productive* conflict, you won't need the facilitator for every issue—you will know how to handle it on your own, as a team.

Another option is to bring in someone to speak to your team about communication and conflict. Look for someone who can provide general strategies and suggestions. You don't need someone who is going to tell you communication is important and that gossip is bad. You know that. Your team needs information on what to do about it.

Find the Best Solution for Your Team

Pushing conflict down until it explodes is a common, but ineffective, way to deal with a problem. If there is no conflict on a team, someone is either lying or hiding the truth. It is much better to develop an agreed-upon plan and deal with issues when they are small and manageable. Sometimes it takes a trained facilitator to help develop and teach this process, but the dividends of having it will pay well into the future by reducing (or even eliminating) drama as the method used to address conflict. The benefits of these skills do not end with your team—they will be used long into the future with friends, parents, siblings, and coworkers.

As a team, talk about which of the above solutions are likely to work best for you and try them. Don't be afraid to mix and match. The whole point is to create a solution that works for your team and it will be unique to your team. It has been shown that individuals who *trust* each other have less relationship conflict. Cognitive conflict develops understanding and improves communication, which will increase trust. To be more successful in all of your endeavors, reduce relationship conflict by eliminating character attacks and gossip. Discuss informational differences by sharing where you stand and how you feel about something using "I" statements. If you can own your own thoughts and feelings while listening to the thoughts and feelings of others, that skill will take you far.

Recognizing and Addressing Emotional Bullying

I could hear the giggling and not-so-quiet whispering across the room. A few words escaped their circle: "stupid", "ugly", "can't play", "should quit", and finally, my name. Of course they were talking about me. They were, after all, volleyball players, and I was new to the school, new to the game of volleyball. My father thought it would be a good idea for me to join a sport as a way to make friends. All it accomplished was to teach me that the volleyball team was a bunch of mean girls who were more interested in makeup than in being athletes. It certainly didn't do me any favors that most of them struggled to keep their grades up to be eligible to play while I got A's—I had just replaced one of them as a starter because she was failing classes.

Did they really not know I was in the room, or did they just not care if I heard them being hateful? They didn't talk to me like that on the court. In fact, they acted like they wanted to help me be a better player. I just sat there listening to them, feeling more and more hurt and alone.

* * *

Emotional bullying, clinically called *relational aggression,* is the act of attacking someone's feelings and the relationships they have with other people. Typical outlets for emotional bullying are gossip, rumors, and outright lies. This type of bullying can happen in person, on Facebook, via text, and over email. If you think only teenage girls engage in such behavior, think again. There is evidence of it as early as grade school and it is rampant in the workforce.

Tearing other people down rather than building oneself up is often used to try to level the playing field. Unfortunately, it works. When we hear negative information from someone we trust about someone we do not know, or know only in passing, we believe it. Rather than taking the time to gather our own information, we take the easy road and go with what we hear. Not very fair, but it is what we do.

Many coaches, athletes, parents, and administrators just give up. They say things like, "There is nothing I can do. Girls are just like that." "Our team just has a bad apple. We will have to wait it out until she graduates." "This team is cliquey and just won't work together."

But, we have more control than we think. Bullies—emotional or otherwise—are given their power by the team. The team has the ability to remove that power, too; they just need to take a stand. When teams commit to consistently bringing power back to the whole group using the following ideas, a bully will either come in line with the group or go find other people to bully.

Are you a bully?

You need to be certain that you don't engage in bullying yourself. I know you are thinking, "Of course I don't bully!" Because you picked up and are reading this book, maybe you are self-aware enough that you don't. However, double check:

> *Are you ever guilty of pushing your weight around to get your way rather than talking something through like you should?*
>
> *Do you talk and laugh with your friends and ignore people you don't know?*
>
> *Do you find sharing the shortcomings of others great fun "just for laughs"?*

You may think of those types of behaviors the same way you think about white lies: "I'm not really hurting anyone." But, in fact, you *are*.

You are setting the stage for emotional bullying to be acceptable. The line between fun teasing and bullying is vague and drawn in different places for different people. If you don't engage in any teasing or hurtful banter, you won't have to worry about where that line is, and you will have the integrity to call someone out when they go too far.

Bringing power back to the group

Don't allow bullying to take place around you. When you hear someone say something mean, act hatefully, or tear others down but say nothing, *your silence is agreement*. I am not saying you need to get into a verbal fray about every bullying statement you hear, but simply saying, "That isn't a very nice thing to say" or "I don't agree" will make it clear that you do not condone that behavior. You can go even further by saying, "It is not okay with me for you to talk like that about other people."

Be compassionate and teach others compassion. It really isn't that difficult to be nice. Check in with people; ask how they are doing. If you hurt someone's feelings, apologize. I'm pretty sure most mothers still teach this stuff. Use it. If your friends find it odd to be nice to other people, you have the wrong kind of friends.

Gather your own information about others. Don't take the easy way out by believing whatever you hear—find out the truth for yourself. If it turns out the person really is a jerk, you can be confident that you learned it firsthand rather than through hearsay.

Hold yourself and others accountable to the rule that if someone has a problem with someone else, they need to have a conversation with that person about it. The coach may need to be involved in some situations, but they should not need to be drawn into *every* disagreement. If the team has been given the skills addressed in the previous chapters, have them try to work it out themselves. The coaching staff is not responsible for having all the answers all the time.

Listen. You will hear the rumblings of bullying on your team. All you have to do is pay attention. Don't ignore 'little' things, allowing them to grow into 'big' ones. Address gossip, rumors, and other forms of emotional bullying right away.

Talk to the bully. Calling someone on their inappropriate behavior is one of the hardest, *but most productive,* things you can do. Talk specifically about behaviors that need to change (see Chapter Eight about having tough conversations). Ask questions about what drives those people to behave that way, what they think they are gaining by their actions, and why they target the people they do. If you can gain an understanding about what is going on in their head, you are more likely to be able to create a logical argument against it.

* * *

I went to high school with a girl whose nickname was Amazon. She was big, tall, and strong. Sadly, she was also cruel. One afternoon I walked around a corner to find a large group of people who were yelling mean, hateful, nasty words. Not even complete sentences. "Stupid!" "Ugly!" "Reject!"

As I peered through the crowd, my heart sank. We had a special needs school on our campus and the students were often on the receiving end of bullying. Amazon had her fist clenched on the front of another girl's shirt, pulling her almost off the ground. Amazon was much bigger than me and known to hold grudges, but I couldn't just walk by and let the abuse continue. I knew it was likely to escalate into a physical fight and the smaller girl didn't stand a chance.

With my heart pounding, I stepped into the ring created by the students standing around watching. "Hey!" I yelled. Amazon let go of the other girl and wheeled around. "What is wrong with you that you need to pick on someone so much smaller than you? Does it make you feel big or smart to pick such an uneven fight?" The girl who had been the focus of her wrath saw her chance and bolted through the crowd to the safety of her classroom.

I really had no reason to fight with Amazon. I could beat her at verbal judo, but if she started swinging, I was going to be in trouble. She walked towards me and between her teeth said, "What did you say?"

I shrugged. "I just wondered what you got out of abusing someone so out of your league." I turned and started to walk away. The crowd parted in front of me. I heard her come up behind me. Just loud enough for her to hear me, I growled, "Don't touch me" and kept walking.

I got lucky that day. Amazon just stood there as I walked away. But I have to admit, I kept a wide berth around her after that. Rumor had it that she was out to get me. I had no desire to be "got."

Self-Awareness 101

Self-awareness is a funny thing. If you *don't* have it, you don't know you don't have it and you don't know you need it. When you *do* have it, you know it is very useful when interacting with others, but you can't teach it to someone else. The worst situation involves people who *think* they are self-aware, but really aren't—that is a tough situation for everybody.

So what is self awareness? The simple answer is someone being knowledgeable about how their words and actions affect others. That is wonderful in theory, but often very difficult in practice. Here are some ways you can become more self-aware and how you can gently nudge others to be more observant when words or actions are having a potentially unnoticed negative effect.

Perception vs. Reality

When I do speaking engagements, I often ask, "What is the difference between perception and reality?" Think about that for a moment. What is the difference to you? I get a variety of answers that can be summed up by "Reality is what is really going on. Perception is what someone (usually mistakenly) *thinks* is going on." More often than not, when someone says, "Well, that's your perception", what they are really saying is, "You are clearly dead wrong, but I'll be polite and not throw it in your face."

This leads to my answer to the same question: "Perception is what *you* think. Reality is what *I* think." (To which I usually hear chuckling in response). But it is true—each of us thinks we are the only one in tune with reality. We think everyone else is just floundering around in the world of misperception. The collective truth (the real "reality") is the whole of everyone's perceptions combined—not an easy idea to get your mind around in the abstract, let alone when you are in the moment and living life.

So, what do you do with that information? The only thing you can do is respect that your perception might be as far from the truth as someone else's, and the only way to get to a point of agreement is to have a respectful conversation where each of you explains your take on the situation and listens to what the other person thinks—perfect for using *The Seven No-Fail Secrets to Stop The Drama!*

Emotional intelligence

I was invited to go to dinner by a good friend of mine. The group turned out to be rather large—15 or so people, if I remember correctly. I ended up sitting across from my friend and his sister was seated to his right. Early in the evening we learned that his sister was dealing with a messy break-up from a long-term relationship. I could feel how badly she was hurting as she told the story. Tears slid down her cheeks and soon she was openly sobbing. I wanted to reach across to comfort her, but the table was too wide.

I looked to my friend, expecting to see the same feelings on his face. I was shocked! He was eating his soup and didn't even seem to be noticing! I got his attention and said, "Your sister is crying." He responded, "I know" and kept eating. I waited a few moments and then said, "Comfort her." He looked up from his soup in confusion and replied, "Uh? How?" I know the look on my face must have conveyed my disbelief, "Put your arm around her," I replied. He put down his spoon and awkwardly reached toward her. Before he even touched her, she collapsed into his chest, weeping. He looked uncomfortable and uneasily patted her shoulder.

* * *

What I had observed showed a complete lack of emotional intelligence. Not only did my friend not have the ability to correctly interpret the feelings going on around him, he was clueless as to how to respond to them even when they were pointed out to him.

Of course, this is an extreme example, but I have seen very similar situations on athletic fields. Someone leaves the field obviously frustrated and upset, yet no one from their team checks in with them. A coach completely loses his cool in a meeting and then doesn't understand why everyone tiptoes around him for the rest of the day.

But what is emotional intelligence (EI) really? Understanding and expressing your emotions effectively is part of it. But being able to correctly interpret the feelings of others and respond to them appropriately is the basic foundation of EI.

Being emotionally intelligent starts with *paying attention*. What is going on with the people around me? How do I feel about it? A list of 'feeling' words can be very helpful (one is provided for you in Section Three). If you can't come up with the right word, you won't really understand what is going on. Think it sounds corny? Look at thesaurus.com to see all the different synonyms for 'angry'. There are more than 50 of them, and it doesn't even get into being frustrated or disappointed. Once you have an understanding of the feelings going on, what is the appropriate social response? Are you brave enough to be involved or are you going to play it safe and pretend emotion can be overridden by logic?

This is what I can tell you for certain: emotions have a huge effect on every personal interaction we have. Call it 'going with your gut' or intuition or even try to ignore them; they will influence you one way or another. Fortunately, your level of emotional intelligence is something you can change over time with practice. Sometimes it takes having someone to help point out where you might be lacking, but growth *is* possible. Talking about it with your teammates will allow you to grow together.

Emotional "stuff"

My stuff, your stuff, everybody has stuff. I am not talking about physical stuff we keep in boxes or piles; I am talking about emotional stuff. The hurts, compliments, slaps in the face, and pats on the back that we have accumulated over the years. As we get to know someone, we accumulate ideas about how they treat us and build a box we fit them into.

Each interaction either confirms our existing picture of a person or changes it—for better or worse. The problem is that we are prone to seeing things that fit into the box of who we believe a person is and ignoring things that could change our opinion. Once we think we know a person, they are stuck being the person we believe they are even if it isn't really true. Some people categorize and compartmentalize their emotional stuff while others have it scattered all over their emotional space; most are somewhere in between.

Sometimes we put new people into a box we built for someone else. Your new teammate, Tammy, does something similar to a childhood enemy you once had. In your mind, Tammy suddenly takes on all the characteristics of that person you knew years ago! You just put her into someone else's box.

Regardless of your emotional filing system, or lack thereof, or whom you box with whom, there are going to be days that people are going to stumble into your stuff. When they do, watch out! The reaction they get from you is likely to have nothing to do with what is going on right then—your reaction is going to be based on the "stuff" in that box.

Here is the thing about emotional stuff: we usually want to blame other people for our stuff and accept blame for other people's stuff. It is an odd way to go about life, but if you think about it, it happens every day. Anytime someone starts a sentence with "you made me...." or "I did that because..." followed by something someone *else* did, they are passing off their stuff.

Consider the coach who yells at an athlete and then later says, "I'm sorry I yelled, but you made me angry." Putting aside the fact that an "I'm sorry" should *never* be followed by "but," the coach is telling the athlete, "I gave you control over my emotions. You managed them poorly and made me angry." I don't know about you, but if I were in charge of the coach's emotions, anger would certainly *not* be one I would choose. However, the athlete is likely to have walked away from that conversation thinking, "I have to be more careful to not make Coach angry." The coach packed an emotional box; then the athlete picked it up and carried it out. Now energy that the athlete *could* use to be productive is being siphoned off to working on managing someone else's emotions—an impossible task.

There are two sides to this issue: owning your own stuff and not accepting ownership of the stuff belonging to others. We will look at both.

Owning your own stuff

This seems like it should be pretty simple: you are responsible for your own emotions. But it doesn't tend to work that way. It is much easier to be defensive, blame everyone and anyone, and to walk away feeling morally justified, particularly because feelings are something we never allow to cloud our judgment (yeah, right). Clearly, it must be someone else's fault! That is not the case—it is time to own up and take responsibility for what is yours. That is not to say you can't tell someone how you are reacting to them. Rather than saying, "You did *this* and made me do *that*!" try something like, "I expected you to follow up on my feedback. I am very frustrated that it didn't happen" or "I am offended and resentful that you arrived at training camp overweight and out of shape."

Starting a sentence with "I" instead of "you" takes ownership of your feelings, doesn't assign blame or create a situation where the other person feels like they have to defend themselves against an attack. "I am disappointed" creates space for a conversation, a feeling of 'we are in this together, let's work it out.' "You disappointed me" starts the discussion off with a "me against you" posture which leads to a winner and a loser (and, in too many cases, two losers).

When I work with clients on this topic, I often provide them with a list of 'feelings' words (you can find one in Section Three). You will not be able to own your feelings if you don't understand them, and you can't explain them to others if you can't find the right words.

Not accepting other people's stuff

This one can be tough, too. Accepting blame, fault, or just carrying someone's emotional baggage is a bad habit I see every day. How you handle it depends on the relationship between the people or team involved. If your team has done some team development work and has a common communication fingerprint, you can talk to the person about it.

Maybe you will come to the agreement that you will hold their emotion for a time and then talk about it later (this is an advanced technique). I have often said in team meetings, "Let me hold that worry for now. I promise it will not get lost and we can talk about it later." It is amazing how much it helps a team or an individual when someone else is willing to help them carry an emotional burden. That is not to say I take the blame for how they feel. I just help them understand the feelings and support them. If your team has a way to talk about it, emotional stuff is just one more thing to maintain during a conversation and it builds team trust.

The more challenging situation is when you are using the black box of hope for communication (see Chapter Three for a refresher) hoping it will work. If someone is packing their stuff on you and you don't have a common communication fingerprint, you have two options: one, diffuse—"I can tell you are furious about this situation"; two, protect yourself—if the person simply will not be deterred, let them pack those boxes with their stuff and let them vent. Just remember not to take their box with you when you leave!

Being self-aware and emotionally intelligent means asking yourself and your teammates some tough questions. Are you a master at accepting emotional boxes from people? Maybe you are an emotional shipper. What does that look like? In either case, how would you like the people you trust the most (hopefully your teammates) to point it out to you and help you learn to be more self-aware about the ownership of emotional stuff? Trust me; it is a very beneficial conversation to have.

Successfully Giving and Receiving Feedback

A bigwig from out of town was holding a meeting to get 'feedback' on how things were going in our department. He talked about how we were all crew members on a ship; how it took all of us working together to move forward. I felt like it was a fancy speech. The truth was that we were floundering. Changes where being made too quickly and all of us were running in different directions just trying to keep day-to-day operations functioning. I was frustrated that nobody was listening nor helping us. The decisions being made where making things worse, not better.

When the time came for the team to give him feedback I said, "If we are on a ship, you are on the top deck enjoying a nice jazz band and cocktails. I am in the engine room bailing water!"

Needless to say, my 'feedback' was neither heard nor applied. I hadn't used words that made sense to him. He shut me down by saying, "Oh, come on, it can't be that bad." No one else bothered to explain to him how badly we were struggling or how he could help. He left feeling like things were going pretty well and that I was just a whiner.

* * *

Oh, the dreaded "constructive" criticism. Many people hate giving it because it can easily cause hurt feelings. Others hide behind a veil of being constructive when, in reality, they are just being mean. Being criticized is painful and even getting relatively gentle feedback can be rough. People can become defensive, shut down, and cannot hear what is being said as constructive. Relationships can be strained.

We are taught to be 'nice' and try to never hurt someone's feelings. We might ignore times when we could say something to help someone grow for fear of hurting them. That doesn't build a strong team. Healthy teams love each other enough to give the tough feedback and trust each other enough to apply it. I know a team who hung that on their locker room wall. But how do you get there? By having the emotional guts to try.

Getting honest feedback

It's a standard joke: "Do these pants make my butt look fat?" "No, not at all." When in reality the truth is something closer to "OMG! Did she even look in the mirror?" Why do we do that? Why do we ask when we don't want the truth and why do we lie even when someone might really want to know the truth?

Once again, we are trying to be nice. But is it really nice to lie to someone? Clearly, no. So it isn't that we are trying to be nice; we are actually trying to avoid conflict. We are often much more interested in keeping the peace than getting the truth out in the open. But there are some ways we can make it safe for people to tell us the truth:

> ***Don't ask for feedback you don't really want.*** Fishing for compliments will get you just that—compliments, not the truth. If you don't want to hear that your coaching style is harsh, don't ask.

If you would rather your teammates let you keep making the same mistake over and over, don't ask them to help you correct it.

When someone is brave enough to give you feedback, listen. Pay attention to your physical response. If you are becoming defensive, ask yourself why. You are being offered an opinion. Even if the person speaks as though they are stating fact, it is really just their opinion—you are allowed to accept it or not. The more defensive you feel, the more likely you should consider that what they are saying may actually have some merit.

Make it safe to tell you the truth. Too often we attack the person (relationship conflict) when we don't like the message (informational conflict). Instead, ask for more information. Can they give you specific examples of behaviors or actions which led them to the opinion they have? Can they suggest specific things you could adjust? Generalizations can be the death of good communication. For example: someone once provided the feedback that I was "too loud." That is a very broad statement—too loud when? always? right now? in meetings? in general conversation? As it turned out, the person wasn't so much concerned about the volume of my speech as she was about the emotional intensity with which I was discussing a specific topic. If I had not followed up on her comment, I would have simply lowered my volume and thought she should be happy.

We are really good at making it clear when we are not interested in the information being provided. If you are defensive, aggressive, rude, or generally treat someone badly after they try to give you feedback, they will notice. Other people who observe the exchange will notice, too, and it will get shared with the team. In time, you will become like a leader atop a crumbling company—the pillars are collapsing but only good news is being filtered to the top. If you want the truth, create an environment where it is safe to tell the truth, even when it is bad news.

Use the feedback you are given. No one likes to feel like they are putting their neck on the line for nothing. When someone gives you feedback and it appears you ignored it, they (and others) will not bother to approach you again. That is not to say every bit of feedback must translate to a change on your part—not at all—but it does require a response of some kind. Make the speaker feel heard (see Chapter Seven). Make sure you understand what it is they are trying to tell you. Then, give yourself some time to think about it. Finally, decide if you believe it is something you need to change or if there is a valuable reason to keep things as they are. By the way, the answers "I have always been that way" and "This is just how we have always done it" are prime reasons to consider making a change.

I was at a conference when I heard, "The Stone Age didn't end for lack of stones." That is an amusing way to say that there might be something better than what you have always done. If you decide change is not necessary, explain to the person that you heard what they had to say and why you disagree (without putting them down). A teammate who feels like you heard their point of view, but disagreed, will be much happier than one who feels like you didn't listen to them at all.

Giving honest feedback

Shannon, a national-level competitive cross-country skier had a coach, Carol, who was one of her best friends for many years. Over the course of several months, Shannon noticed that Carol was spending less and less time coaching her at practice. After a particularly hard fall during a competition, Carol walked over, smacked Shannon on the backside, and made a comment that Shannon thought was rude—and she made it loudly enough that members of other teams heard it.

Shannon was mortified when a coach from another team came over and asked if she was alright and why she allowed her coach to treat her so badly. The final straw came when Shannon was giving Carol some used equipment for the team to use and Carol said, "I see you're off-loading your junk on me again." Shannon felt unappreciated and abused not only as an athlete, but as a friend. When asked why she didn't say anything, Shannon's response was, "I have seen how she is. If I try to talk to her, she will be mean and blow me off anyway. I don't want to deal with the conflict." Shannon quit the team and is no longer in contact with her former friend and coach.

* * *

I don't know Carol's side of the story. But let's think about it for a moment. What explanations could there be for her actions? Maybe she didn't realize she was ignoring Shannon. Maybe there were some unconscious feelings that Shannon was performing better than Carol had at her own competitive peak and she resented it, but didn't realize it was showing in her coaching. Maybe she thought their friendship was such that smacking her backside was encouraging. Maybe she was teasing about the "junk." The thing is, we will never know, because Shannon never initiated the conversation to find out. She quit the team and no longer has Carol as a friend. Could the outcome have been much worse if she had asked what was going on? If she knew how to manage the emotions and find out the facts, it might have ended the same way, but at least Shannon would know.

Giving feedback can be even more daunting than receiving it. You want to be honest; you really need to say something. But what to say, how to say it, and the risk that it will be taken the wrong way and turned into a nasty disagreement makes it easier to say nothing at all. If you approach the situation in the right way—knowing what you want to say and saying it from a place of caring—you are much more likely to have a positive outcome. Here are a few things to consider when you want to give someone feedback:

Why do you want to provide the feedback? Understanding your motivation is important. Being judgmental, critical, or mean should never be justified as being feedback. Using the label "constructive criticism" does not provide a carte blanche to be hurtful. If you can *honestly* say that your goal is to better the relationship, help someone change self destructive behaviors, or protect yourself from emotional, psychological, or physical harm, then feedback is the way to go.

How does the behavior you want to see changed make you feel? You might need to consult the feelings words list for this one (See Section Three). If someone isn't pulling their weight at practice, you may feel disappointed or perhaps concerned about their well-being (are they injured or is something going on that is affecting their focus?). In the example above, Shannon could feel taken advantage of or unappreciated. Take the time to figure out how you feel. If you don't know, and can't put it into words, you are certainly not going to be able to explain it.

What are the logistics of the conversation? Where should it take place? I worked with a team that set up a team rule stating they were not allowed to give each other feedback in the shower after one member jerked a shower curtain open and said, "I need to talk to you!" to a stunned teammate who had shampoo in her hair. It should go without saying that is *not* a good way to approach a conversation! So think about what would be best for you and for the person you need to talk to. Nobody likes to be embarrassed, so initiating a conversation in front of other teammates is probably *not* the best option. Pick a time and a place when she is least likely to feel defensive.

Start the conversation by asking for her involvement. Bring her into the conversation. You want her to join you; you don't want to just talk *at* her. Teams I have worked with have had success with variations of, "I have something important I'd like to talk to you about. Is now a good time?" This type of opening shows the other person that you respect her, and it gives her a moment to prepare herself to listen to what you have to say.

If it happens to not be a good time, you can follow up by asking when *would* be good for her. This works particularly well on teams with an established communication fingerprint because both parties know what to expect and go into the conversation with a positive mindset.

Start your sentences with "I" not "you." As we've discussed, owning your feelings by saying "I" is much better than blaming someone by saying "you." Placing blame or fault will only create a situation where she feels like she needs to defend herself. Once that happens, it becomes a verbal wrestling match with a winner and a loser. Instead, think of it as dancing—work together to understand each other and come up with a solution that is acceptable to both of you.

Assume the positive. Assume your teammate was not intending to hurt or annoy you and that when you explain how you feel about her actions, she will try to understand. Listen when she responds to you. Maybe you misunderstood her behavior and she can explain it. Maybe she is willing to make a change to better herself or help the team function more smoothly. You won't know if you don't explain and then *listen*.

Know when to call a timeout. In a productive conversation where both parties are working together, you are unlikely to need to call a timeout—but pay attention. If emotions start running high and the conversation has escalated past the point of being helpful, stop it—but don't abandon the subject completely. Instead, explain that you feel like you need more time to think, and schedule time to talk about it again later. If need be, ask someone to help facilitate the conversation—someone you both respect and preferably someone with training in facilitating conflict.

Calling in other teammates, boyfriends, and sometimes even coaching staff may not be the best plan. If your team doesn't have an unbiased support person (sport psychologist, counselor, even academic advisors can be helpful) now might be a good time to bring the need to the attention of the coaching staff or administration. Never let a timeout turn into 'ignored.' She who calls a timeout is responsible for making sure the conversation is continued later.

Remember, you cannot change someone else. You can control yourself, your reactions, and the situations you put yourself in, but you cannot control other people. If you talk to someone and they are unwilling to see the damage they are causing, look at the components that can be controlled. What can you do differently? If you don't like the response you are getting, change your dance step—your partner then will have to change theirs.

Having a plan and a desired outcome will go a long way toward helping you find your voice so you can discuss even tough subjects (see Chapter Eight for more on having tough conversations). I will repeat the motto I shared earlier in the chapter: *Love each other enough to give tough feedback; trust each other enough to use it.*

Know Yourself, Know Your Team

Being part of a great team means feeling supported and being able to support your teammates. Have you ever thought about what makes you feel supported? Do you know for sure what your teammates need from you when they are stressed? On most teams, the answer to both of those questions is 'no'. That is easy to fix. It just takes figuring it out by having the conversation.

* * *

A teammate of mine recently went through a tough period in her life. I often heard her say how alone and overwhelmed she felt. I thought that was strange because I know she has lots of friends who always said, "If you need anything, call me." I was guilty of doing the same thing. I would end conversations with, "You know if you need anything, I'm here for you."

It took me much longer than I would like to admit to figure out that she was so overwhelmed that she didn't even know what she needed and therefore couldn't ask. It finally came to light that the way to help was to make sure she ate. Knowing she would have healthy food to eat and she didn't have to think about it, was huge for her. Once she realized that she was able to ask for that help from her friends, it made a big difference in her stress level.

But why didn't she just ask for it before? There were several of us who would have been happy to bring food over or go out with her. All she had to do was say the word. The truth, though, was that she was too stressed out to even analyze what kind of help she wanted or needed.

* * *

How well do you know you?

It seems like a pretty straightforward question. Of course the answer is 'you know yourself better than anyone else does.' Now, here is a more difficult question: how well can you explain 'you' to other people? Being able to do that requires taking your overall belief of who you are and put it, honestly, into words. That is more complex than it sounds. Psychology studies have shown it is common for people to tell others who they *wish* they were rather than who they *really* are. Not because they are mean-spirited and lying, but because the desire to be something is so strong that they believe they really *are* who they *want* to be. This means maybe you don't know yourself as well as you think you do.

Here are a few great personal and team development questions to help you learn a little bit about yourself and each other. (Note: If you try to get team members who don't trust each other to share this type of information, they will lie to make themselves looks good. That totally defeats the purpose of the exercise. Build the trust *first* and come back to this exercise if you need to.)

How do you want to receive feedback? If you are like most people, how you want others to talk to you has never specifically crossed your mind. But, when someone does it wrong, you certainly recognize it and become hurt or angry. So, if someone has something they want to discuss with you, what is the best way to approach you?

Here are a few examples I have heard from clients to get you started:

> "Feedback works best for me one on one, in private. When someone gives me feedback and other people can hear it, I feel criticized and am quick to become defensive. Once that happens, I have a hard time taking it in and using what is being said."

> "I am pretty good at hearing feedback as feedback when it is coming from someone I trust. When I know someone, it's cool if they just say, "hey, do it this way," but if it is somebody I don't really know, it is better if they pull me aside."
>
> "I have a pretty tough skin and I'm all about getting better. If someone sees something I can improve, I want them to speak up right away. That way I have context for what they are telling me. After the fact, I won't be able to apply it."
>
> "I know I'm a softie when it comes to being told I'm doing something wrong. I feel like a failure and stupid. I am working on not shutting down when people try to help me get better... I guess for me it works best if my teammates know to be nice about it. I want feedback. I want to get better. It is just something I can use some help with."

After a discussion about how each team member prefers to receive feedback, you will have a better understanding about each other's (and hopefully your own) individual communication fingerprint. But how will you or one of your teammates know when someone needs help? What are the signs that someone is crashing and burning before things are totally out of control? Those things vary from person to person, too! That means figuring it out and sharing it with each other.

Questions you can think about individually and discuss as a team include:

> *What are the top two or three things in your life where you feel the most pressure to complete them to the very best of your ability?* Is it acing that exam? Running a six-minute mile? Finding the perfect internship? Landing the ideal recruit? It doesn't matter how important it seems in the "grand scheme" of things—this is about what is important to you.

Who are the two or three people in your life who will always have your back? You know the old saying, "Good friends help you move. Great friends help you move bodies." Of course I am not suggesting you will be moving a body! But those are the kind of friend you turn to in crisis. Knowing who you can call at 2am if your world is falling apart is important. Who are those people and how do they support you? What do they do that makes you feel supported? What makes them the "go-to" people in your life?

What does being overstressed look and feel like for you? In other words: how will you know when you need to ask for support before it is too late? A feeling of overall muscle tightness, being unable to sleep and jumping from project to project without finishing anything are common responses (too much to do in too little time). What is it for you? No one expects you to be superwoman. Share what you look like when your life starts to feel crazy so your teammates can recognize when they should offer help.

Put all the pieces together. Talk to the people who love and care about you (on and off the team). Share what it looks like when you are walking that thin line between holding it together and losing it. Tell them the things that are most important for you to get done. That way, the next time you need someone, you won't get the broad, "Let me know what I can do" response—instead, they will know that bringing dinner, helping you study, or running that extra mile with you is the kind of support you need. And not only that, when someone asks, "How can I help?" you will know what to ask for so you can keep your energy up and continue to get the most from your potential!

Having a better understanding of what makes you tick and how you perceive the world is never a bad thing. Sharing it with your teammates will give them the insight they need to support you in the way that works best for you. Knowing how to best encourage your teammates will give you the confidence to know your energy is not being wasted when you are trying to help. Together, this knowledge will make you a stronger, more cohesive team that will work through personal challenges as well as performance and emotional lows quickly and move on to greater success.

How Does Your Team Handle Confidentiality?

The father of an athlete stood next to me on the grass after the game. He was smiling, but I could feel the undercurrent of annoyance. His daughter, Stacie, had been pulled out of the game and replaced by a freshman, but that didn't seem to be the source of his aggravation.

He said, "Stacie talked to Lara (the assistant coach) in confidence. Lara had no business taking that information to the head coach."

I knew this team. I knew there was an understanding that anything said to one coach would be shared with the coaching staff. I had been involved in the meeting where that norm had been expressly discussed. I asked, "Why did Stacie think the conversation would be kept private?"

He replied, "The conversation was about the head coach and Lara had a few choice words to say herself. She certainly wouldn't want Stacie sharing what she said with the head coach."

He had a fair point. An assistant coach engaging in coach bashing with a player would certainly create the assumption of confidentiality which could override the established rule. I later learned that Stacie had confronted Lara in a meeting with the entire coaching staff and Lara had ended up in tears. Not a good ending for anyone.

* * *

Every team I have ever worked with has had challenges with regard to confidentiality. Feelings of breached trust or regrets about secrets are common. However, very few teams actually discuss when privacy becomes secrecy or when transparency turns into gossip. Taking the time to create guidelines and set expectations will eliminate the vague use of individual discretion and provide a firm foundation for everyone to know where they stand.

Confidentiality is relevant in three distinct team relationships: coach to coach, coach to athlete, and athlete to athlete. Many teams have additional relationships with an athletic trainer or academic counselor. Each comes with its own pitfalls, risks and rewards, assumptions, and broken promises. Even when there is an established way that confidentiality is supposed to work, athletes and coaches can accidently create the belief that the instituted standard has been suspended. These misunderstandings can lead someone to believe that confidentiality exists when it doesn't or to share things they should not. Rather than leaving the whole mess-up to chance and hoping for the best, work with your team to develop expectations around how confidentiality fits into your team communication fingerprint.

Coach-to-Coach

It is a given that coaches talk behind closed doors about things that are not meant for the ears of their athletes, administration, and coaches of other teams. A coaching staff spends a lot of time together. They get comfortable with each other, and whether they are just blowing off steam, discussing whether an athlete should start, or being annoyed that facilities can't seem to schedule their way out of a wet paper bag, there is often an assumption of confidentiality. Reputations have been ruined by that assumption. It is just as important for a coaching staff to talk about confidentiality as it is for players.

The best place to start is to know where you stand on confidentiality personally. Once you know what you expect of others, you can compare and discuss it with the rest of the staff and the athletes. These questions will help start the discussion:

What topics are assumed to be confidential? Should they be? Why or why not?

What is the expectation if an athlete, parent, another coach, the administration, etc. speaks to one member of your staff? Is the conversation confidential, should it be shared with the staff, or does it depend on the situation? (I strongly suggest not leaving things in the "depends" category; there is too much room for misunderstanding and error.)

Is it okay for two members of the coaching staff to get together to vent about another member of the staff? What is the expectation of how someone should handle it if they find themselves in a situation where one person is complaining about another?

What about talking to friends or significant others about work? Does location matter? Is asking the outsider to keep it to themselves expected? This is particularly important for high-profile coaches. People need to be able to talk about work, but doing so in a crowded restaurant at a table of ten might not be the best plan.

How does your team handle talking to the press?

How does confidentially play into your recruiting process? Too often secrets are kept from recruits because the information might put the team in a bad light. But is lying, even by omission, the stage you want to create for your team?

Of course, add topics to this list as you see fit. The point of the exercise is to open the discussion so everyone can be on the same page about the confidentiality expected within the coaching staff. If you never talk about it, you have no standard to measure for accountability. You will have no way of knowing that your expectation of confidentiality is different from someone else's until it becomes a problem.

Coach-to-Athlete

Coaches talk to athletes, athletes talk to coaches, and the line of authority can become blurred with friendship. This can be a particular problem in the college setting where assistant coaches are often only a couple of years older than the athletes. Young women need a place they believe is safe to confide stress and anxiety. Girls in tears over boyfriends, grades, parents, siblings, friends, playing time, performance, teachers, and any host of other subjects is a normal occurrence. As their coach, you want to listen and help them, and—to a great extent—it is part of the job. The question is: now that you have all that information, what will you do with it? Athletes usually assume those sessions are completely confidential; maybe most of them are. But what if the athlete is really in trouble, if it is more than just the pains of life? Do you call parents, involve a counselor, tell other coaches or the police? No doubt it is a judgment call. Do you, your coaching staff, and your athletes know where that line is drawn? Setting expectations in this case is very important.

Athletic Trainer/Academic Counselors/Other Staff

If your team has an athletic trainer, this is another relationship to consider. I have spoken to athletic training groups and I hear how they feel like they need a degree in psychology to deal with the emotional needs of their athletes. As a coach, what is your expectation of getting information—emotional or otherwise—from the trainer? As an athlete, do you believe the only information being passed to your coach is about your physical condition and anything else talked about is confidential?

If it is an option, you may consider having someone on your staff who is a confidante for the team. It is a role I have played many times and I have heard from coaches how much it relieves them of trying to be a therapist. Someone trained for that type of responsibility is going to be able to establish where the lines of confidentially are drawn. They also may be better equipped to recognize the difference between when someone is just releasing tension and when they are really in trouble and asking for help. If you have access to a sport psychologist, this might be a role he or she can fill.

Keep in mind that information doesn't travel only one direction. Athletes do give coaches and other staff members information they may expect will be kept in confidence. But coaches and administration are not immune to sharing private information. When a coach talks to an athlete about his or her frustration with another member of the coaching staff or significant other, it creates a feeling of in-groupness (us versus them).

An authority figure who shares personal information will either make the subordinate feel special for being confided in or powerful for having information perceived to be private which could be used at a later date. In the case of the former, the athlete may believe a special friendship exists and that the agreement that anything shared with one coach will be passed on to the others is waived (as in the case between Stacie and Lara). This creates a misunderstanding about the use of the information in the future.

In a situation where the athlete feels empowered, the coach may later be embarrassed when the shared information becomes public to the team or other coaches. In more serious circumstances, blackmail can become an issue. In either case, it is wise for members of the coaching staff to be prudent about how and where they share their thoughts and feelings about members of the team and the coaching staff.

Athlete-to-Athlete

Confidentiality between athletes is often a challenging topic for coaches to negotiate. But the point of athlete-to-athlete confidentiality is that it does *not* involve the coaching staff. If you have a team development person working with your team, this is a great topic for them to work on with the athletes. There are some things which are very important for the coaching staff to hear—other things, not so much. But leaving to chance the decision of where that line is will lead to hurt feelings, someone being labeled a tattle-tail or an informant, and an overall distrust between team members. This will undermine all of the team building you are trying to do.

Athletes need to be able to talk to each other about things that bother them and feel safe to encourage each other to take important issues to the coaching staff themselves. Having a 'mole' who shares locker room chatter with the coaching staff will create distrust and fractures within the team. It is a topic teammates need to negotiate on their own, because only the team can decide on a norm and hold each other accountable to it.

* * *

JJ (the team captain) and Becky were in the locker room after practice. JJ noticed that Becky was rotating her shoulder and wincing.

JJ: "Hey, what's up with your shoulder?"

Becky: "It's nothing. I just tweaked it a few days back."

JJ: "Doesn't look like nothing. Have you had the trainer look at it?"

Becky: "No, I don't want her to tell Coach, because he'll pull me from practice."

JJ: "It's our responsibility as athletes to take care of our bodies. You really need to see the trainer and talk to Coach."

* * *

JJ is in a tough spot. As the captain of the team, she has responsibility to the team as well as to the coach. There is also an expectation that each athlete is supposed to listen to their bodies and seek medical attention if they are injured. Players often try to hide injuries, sometimes serious ones, so they can be seen as tough and able to work with pain. What should JJ do in this case? If she tells the coach, she will be seen as a nark and the team may ostracize her. If she lets it slide and Becky really ends up hurt, she will have failed her responsibility as a leader on the team. In the best case scenario, the team has already talked about situations like this and JJ isn't left struggling with how to handle it on her own.

Let's say the team decided they handle something like this by being supportive. JJ could say, "How about I go with you to see the trainer? Then we could find out what is going on with your shoulder and how important it is. If need be, I'll go with you to talk to Coach and we can explain how you don't want to miss any practice. Maybe it really is just a tweak. I just don't want to see it really be something serious and have you hurt for the season when maybe you could rest it and solve the issue now."

This type of situation comes up again and again. Athletes live, go to class, socialize, and practice together. They are going to learn the good, the bad, and the ugly about each other. Sometimes the coaching staff should be told and sometimes it really is just a private issue that shouldn't be shared. I have seen issues having to do with missing class, breaking team rules (often around drinking or going out), dating someone's ex, seeing someone's boyfriend out with someone else, skipping practice, and family abuse. The list is endless.

It is always better for the athlete involved to be encouraged by her teammates to share important information herself rather than being tattled on by someone else. Coaches must make every effort not to encourage tattling as it undermines the foundation of trust needed for athletes to build a healthy, high-performing team.

One of the rules I highly encourage teams to adopt is a no-gossip rule. If an athlete has an issue or knows something about another athlete, they need to speak directly to the person involved. If they start talking to someone else, the third party needs to ask, "Have you talked to her about it? I think it is important that you do."

Creating open expectations with regard to when a confidence should and will be *kept* versus when information should and will be *shared* is key to a healthy team. The only way that happens is to talk about it. Figure out where you stand and then set up time to talk to your team!

MY COMMUNICATION PLAYBOOK

Chapter Seven
Communication is the Heart of Success

Let's not forget that the little emotions are the great captains of our lives and we obey them without realizing it.

–Vincent Van Gogh

A lie can be half way around the world before the truth has its boots on.

–James Callaghan

The real art of conversation is not only to say the right thing in the right place, but to leave unsaid the wrong thing at a tempting moment.

–Dorothy Nevill

* * *

Creating a Team Vocabulary

I knew from the phone conversation with the head coach that I was meeting a team who was high on conflict, low on resolution. Among the questions I asked the coaching staff was how they communicated expectations. I was told they were very clear on their expectations and then was handed a code of conduct. This is an excerpt of the expected behaviors:

> *"In meetings, eye contact should be maintained with the speaker at all times.*
>
> *"Eating in meetings is not permitted.*

"Leaving a team meeting before the end is not permitted (make time to use the bathroom before we start or wait until we are done).

"All emails must be responded to within six hours.

"All text or phone messages require an in-kind response indicating you received and understand the message. Email is not an appropriate response to text or phone messages.

"When a member of the coaching staff is speaking, athletes are expected to be silent."

The list continued for about a page-and-a-half. This was a team of college-aged women, so I was shocked to see a document outlining behaviors in such detail. I wondered how the team felt about the minutia of instructions—and it didn't take me long to find out.

After meeting with the coaches, they introduced me to the team. The energy in the room was tense. Questions were responded to only when they were directed to a specific individual. General, open-ended questions were left hanging in silence.

When the coaches left, I explained who I was and that anything the athletes said to me was confidential. I started by asking for their thoughts on the code of conduct, and it didn't take very long for the floodgate of pent-up emotion to fly open: the team said they felt like they were being treated like children.

Words like "insulting", "rude", "disrespectful" were used. One person said, "She wants us to respect *her*, but she doesn't respect *us* at all." There was the crux of the issue. Respect is a word that often means different things to different people.

In this case, the solution we created had three parts:

First, I sat down with the coaches and worked through why they thought they needed such a stringent list; what incident or series of incidents inspired it; how they felt it was working for them; and if they were open to other options;

Next, I worked with the athletes to create a code of conduct they thought was more fitting and met the needs of their team;

Finally, the coaching staff and athletes worked together to define 'respect' and create an agreed-upon code of conduct.

By the end of the process, the team was happier and the coaches felt much more respected.

* * *

The ability for a team to communicate effectively starts with them speaking a common language. I am not talking about whether they speak Spanish, French, or English (although that is very helpful, of course!). I am talking about how words are actually used—how inflection, body language, and tone can change the meaning of a word.

As mentioned in Chapter Three, each player arrives with an individual communication fingerprint—certain words have specific meanings. Players from South Carolina may use words that an athlete from California has never even heard. If you are fortunate enough to have an international recruit, you will learn very quickly that even if they can speak English, it does not guarantee that you will understand what they mean when they put words together (and vice versa).

On-the-field communication is another place where feelings can be hurt accidently and rifts can be created between team members. In the heat of competition, a player may scream "*Now!*" in demand of a pass, or "You need to fill that gap!" as the ball escapes the defense. Frustration can lead to negative comments with no value, such as, "You should have come out of the blocks faster," or "You should have picked a more difficult dive for that heat." Misunderstandings arise; athletes feel attacked rather than supported by their teammates; hurt feelings fester; and the seeds of distrust start to grow.

Teams that discuss on-the-field communication and create short phrases or words that can be used to express concerns or issues that arise on a regular basis will have less conflict over misunderstandings. For example:

There was a coach who was very particular about her athletes being focused during practice. If they were too chatty or didn't move quickly enough between drills, she would make the whole team run wind sprints after practice—one 50-yard sprint for each person caught slacking off. On more than one occasion, a team member trying to quiet someone who was talking out of turn had been tagged for an infraction. The issue was the team was trying to be covert about hushing each other, because they didn't want the coach to notice and handout sprints. However, because the coach couldn't hear what was being said, she just assumed everyone in a group was breaking the rule and handed out more sprints than she otherwise might have.

To solve this problem, we came up with something the athletes could say out loud that was encouraging and that each of them knew meant "focus on practice or we are going to be running sprints." They started and ended practice with a team clap and cheer so they came up with "Wait for the clap." After implementing this particular piece of team vocabulary, the number of extra wind sprints they had to run decreased dramatically.

Another team had a perpetual problem of infighting during games. As long as they were playing well and winning, everything was fine. But if they started making mistakes or were behind on the scoreboard, things would deteriorate into finger-pointing, screaming at one another, or the 'silent treatment.' The bus ride home after losses would start with stony silence and end with the coach having to break up screaming matches about whose fault it was that they lost.

Their problem was twofold: they evaluated their performance during the game (for why that is a problem and how to solve it, see Chapter Ten), and there was a misunderstanding about what and how information was communicated on the field.

One of the captains on this team was a very good player and had great vision on the field—she could see a play unfolding much faster than many of her teammates. During games she would scream things like, "Give me the ball *now!*" "Move to your right, *move to your righ*t!" or "*Fill that gap!*" When they were winning, her teammates where able to just shrug and deal with it. They all respected that she was a good player and her screaming didn't matter when they ended up with a "W." However, when they were losing, the screaming would get more intense and sound more like an attack. Her teammates would feel like she was blaming them and they became defensive, which led to the awful bus rides.

To solve this issue, the captain in question talked at length with the team about the intent of her instructions during games. As it turned out, she wasn't blaming, she was trying to help. She also admitted that her voice became very demanding and hurtful when she was in a pressure situation. She committed to working on that, and her teammates agreed to be more tolerant of her tone.

Finally, they created words and phrases they could use during games to communicate specific information. For when they felt like they were playing back on their heels in a flighty, unorganized fashion, they chose *"Settle!"* When they needed to bring up the intensity: *"Pressure!"* And when someone saw a play or a passing lane, developing players were expected to yell the name of the player who should get the ball.

While watching them play after they created their team vocabulary, I could hear single words and players' names being yelled throughout the game. One parent remarked it was like they had their own language. I just smiled because I knew, win or lose, the bus ride home was going to be fine.

Your Team's Vocabulary

To create your own team vocabulary, brainstorm situations when miscommunication is causing hurt feelings. Are there issues that repeat themselves over and over but never get resolved? Do you have lots of rules that include specific behaviors? Are there team or coach expectations that are consistently not being met? Do the coaches find themselves doling out more punishments than praise?

Those types of issues are a great place to start a conversation about creating and defining vocabulary. Remember, these words are for you and your team. They don't have to even be real words. As long as everybody knows what they mean and they communicate what needs to happen—go ahead and make up some words!

Don't Shoot the Messenger

A very long time ago, messages were written on scrolls, rolled up, sealed with hot wax, imprinted with a ring, and delivered by someone, in person, who had no idea what the message said. The receiver (usually some high and mighty king or similar aristocrat) would give the messenger a really nice gift for good news and punish or even kill him if the news was bad. It was certainly a risky way to make a living for the messenger.

Today the idea of killing someone for delivering bad news is as outdated as sealing scrolls with wax. And, of course, a champion performer like you would never 'shoot the messenger' because you know it stifles communication. Right? Okay, sure we know, and of course we never mean to take our feelings out on the person delivering the message. But sometimes it happens and we don't even realize we are doing it.

When a major issue explodes, we tend to blame the person telling us for not coming forward with the truth sooner. If anyone has ever said, "You are preaching to the choir", you might consider that you were taking your frustration out on the wrong person. Maybe they "should have" come to you sooner. So why didn't they? Simply put, the environment did not feel safe enough for them to share bad news, or maybe they simply didn't have the information earlier. If you want people to come to you with information as soon as they know it, you must figure out what is making it unsafe for them to do so.

* * *

A friend of mine was complaining that her college-aged daughter never told her anything anymore. I asked how she generally felt about the things she wanted to know: she didn't like the boy her daughter was dating, she didn't like her staying out so late, she didn't like how little time she spent studying. The "I don't like" list went on and on. I asked, "Is there anything your daughter could tell you the truth about that you would like?" There was a long pause. "No, I guess not."

Hmm, if every time she opens her mouth she gets a speech about what she is doing wrong, it is no wonder she keeps her life to herself.

* * *

The same situation plays out on teams. If every time someone tells you about a problem they end up involved in a discussion about how things got there (in other words, who is at fault and what should have been done differently), they are going to try everything possible to either fix or hide the problem before coming to you. Worse, the other members of the team will learn from observation to do the same thing. In their heads, a little voice will say, "Note to self: bury as much bad news as possible or risk being blamed." Of course, that is bad for you, bad for the team, and bad for the athletic organization.

Instead of berating the person, try helping them grow. In a bad situation, the best thing you can do is figure out where things *are* (not how they got there) and then develop solutions. *After* the problem has been solved, look into what happened and find ways to develop the knowledge, skills, and abilities of the people involved to avoid a repeat. When coaches, captains, and other team leaders are better at solving problems and teaching solutions rather than judging, team members will feel much safer bringing up concerns before they are out-of-control problems. *You can't judge and solve at the same time.*

Here is a short list of behaviors I have seen which can create a culture of hiding problems. If you think you never do any of them, ask someone who loves you enough to tell you the real truth. I bet you have a couple you could work on. You probably aren't hiding that negative reaction as well as you think you are.

Rolling eyes • Exhaling heavily (huffing) • Judging • Being defensive • Blaming • Evaluating • Refusing to help • Humiliating someone • Giving the "are you really that stupid" look • Going into "you should have…" mode • Giving the silent treatment • Calling someone stupid • Pulling someone out of a play without offering guidance • Wishing a former team member was still around to "do things right" • Taking someone out of the starting line without feedback • Not inviting someone to meetings • Giving the cold shoulder • Leaving someone out of the loop by "accident."

This list could go on and on. Can you think of a behavior your teammates or coaches do that makes you want to hide problems for as long as you can? I bet they think you have some, too! *Talk* about them. Then commit to working on the behaviors that were brought up.

You Can't Observe Why

Bev had hurt her knee in the second match of her junior season. Prior to her injury she was one of the strongest emotional leaders on the team. The thought of doubting her commitment to the team and to the game of tennis never crossed anyone's mind. But now, as the weeks went by with Bev in physical therapy instead of at practice, her teammates started to talk among themselves. "Is she really hurt that bad?" "She can't come to practice *at all?*" "Maybe she's just being lazy and isn't really trying to get back in shape to play."

The truth was that Bev hated being stuck in PT with the trainer. She wanted nothing more than to be out on the courts with her teammates. Every week she begged the trainer and the doctor to clear her to practice, even just a little. With every week that passed without getting clearance, she became more and more sad. She started avoiding her teammates because they were a painful reminder that she couldn't play the sport she was passionate about.

Her teammates and coaches started thinking that maybe she wasn't the player they thought she was. If she wasn't willing to put out the effort to be one of them, they didn't need her anyway. No one called to check in with her and Bev never reached out for the support she so desperately wanted. The emotional gap between a star player and her team grew wider, and it had nothing to do with her knee.

* * *

It is an interesting habit of human nature: our brains always want to know why. If you have ever been around a toddler, you know how often they ask "Why?"...so often that parents become exasperated and simply answer, "Because." As we grow up, we get the message that we aren't supposed to ask 'why' all the time—but that doesn't mean we don't want to know, it just means we don't ask.

When we don't know why someone is doing something (which we usually don't), we make something up. In the example above, why did Bev not come to practice? "She didn't care about the team." "She no longer wanted to play at her previous level."

Why didn't Bev talk to her teammates about how alienated she felt day after day stuck in the training room? "They don't want me." "They don't care about how I'm doing." None of those reasons was the real reason; they were just made-up ones. If either side had bothered to ask why, they would have learned the truth.

When 'why' is made up, it is usually a negative, permanent, and personal attribution: something someone is and always will be. "Bev doesn't come to practice because she doesn't care about our team." That is a very negative, permanent, and personal thing to say. Unless Bev had explicitly said that, how can someone say she (personal) no longer (permanent) cares (negative) about something? That is something only Bev would know.

In contrast, the real reason someone does something is usually neutral, short-term, and situation-specific. Bev's behavior of not being at practice was because she was in PT (neutral) for her injured knee (situation-specific). As soon as she got clearance (short-term) she would be back at practice.

Assuming the Negative

Making up why and assuming negative things can also be applied to conversations. We are programmed to be paranoid. Don't take offence; it is what kept our ancestors alive when there was the very real risk of a deadly beast hiding behind every rock and tree in the landscape. The thing is, unless you are Calvin from the comic strip *Calvin and Hobbes,* you don't have much need to worry about tigers.

Instead, many of us use our paranoid programming to watch out for the coach or teammate who might be 'out to get us.' We take everything they say or do as an indication we are under attack. But the assault isn't really happening, or at least it is being blown out of proportion.

When a teammate does a poor job of bringing up a tough subject and you start to feel attacked, you are assuming the negative and making up a 'why' based on that assumption. Once a negative assumption has been attached, it will cloud how you view someone in the future. If they started out by saying, "I care about you and you are important to me, so I want to talk to you about this issue", they would be providing you with the 'why', so you wouldn't feel the need to make one up—and even if the conversation that followed was difficult, you would be better teammates for it.

We can't always rely on our teammates to let us know when we are making up a 'why' or to bring up conversations in the way that works best for us. We have to take responsibility and catch the thoughts in our head. Those thoughts and feelings are your *internal dialogue.* Learning to be able to monitor it will go a long way to helping you have smooth conversations and a better understanding of your coaches and teammates.

Monitoring your internal dialogue isn't something that can be done by thinking in words. It is about paying attention to your physical reaction to, and feelings about, a situation. What does your body feel like when you are stressed? You might feel pressure in your chest, tightness in your shoulders, maybe your heart rate goes up, or perhaps you start to feel hot. Do you feel negativity such as disappointment, feeling let down, or like someone is not pulling their weight?

Figure out what is going on for you. Once you know what you are looking for, you can start to recognize when you are assuming negative things and making up negative reasons.

When you start to notice your stress reaction and thoughts, you can ask yourself, "What is going on here? Why am I having this reaction or these thoughts?" If you can determine what is causing your body or mind to respond (and that isn't always easy) you will be able to determine if it is something you need to bring up with the team or with an individual. Maybe it is just 'your stuff' and you can deal with it on your own, but you won't know until you can put a label on it.

The next time someone does or says something that annoys you, try to catch yourself as you make up a 'why.' Instead of inventing it out of thin air, *ask* and then *listen*—or at the very least, try assuming something positive. As a team, talk about how you can avoid being ambushed by non-existent tigers. Create a way to talk about those reactions rather than burying them. Trust me, tigers don't like to be buried and the attack will be worse later. Remember, you can observe only the *symptoms* of why someone feels the way they do, and it is very likely that you will misinterpret what you see.

Silence is Golden

Erin, a freshman on the cheerleading squad, stood next to me at the tailgate party after the game. It felt like she had been talking for two minutes straight without taking a breath, which made her frustration ironic.

She ended her little diatribe by saying, "Whenever we have a meeting or talk about something as a squad, everyone is always talking over each other. I can't keep all the different thoughts and ideas straight. Then the coach will say, 'Does anyone have any questions, okay, good.' She never hesitates long enough to let anyone ask a question.

"I feel like I rarely know what goes on in our meetings, so I have to talk to the other girls to find out. But usually everybody has a different idea about what we're supposed to do. It seems like none of us is on the same page. And then Coach told me the other day that I need to step up—that I'm too quiet! *Agh*! Does she want me to *yell* my ideas?"

I smiled. Clearly I needed to explain to the squad why some silence in meetings is a *good* thing.

* * *

Most people hate silence. Athletes are often Type A, highly-driven people and tend to view silence as a waste of time. Nobody is saying anything, thoughts and ideas are not being shared, and therefore nothing is getting done.

Even if you aren't quite that intense about it, silence likely makes you uncomfortable. I am reminded of a boy who was asked to hold a moment of silence for a friend who had died. After about fifteen seconds the boy said, "Okay, that's enough." The crowd chuckled. But I know exactly how the boy felt. Silence is intimidating.

Pay attention the next time you are in a meeting or hanging out with friends. How much silence is there? I would bet almost none (unless the meeting is very tense; but that is a different issue). If someone is always talking, I pose this question: *when is anyone supposed to think?* Clearly the only possible answer is: while someone else is talking.

Now, if I have to think about what I want to say while someone else is talking, who is listening? *Ahh,* now there's the problem: *no one* is listening because when one person is talking, everyone else is thinking about what *they* want to say. No wonder we can't communicate!

Something else to consider when thinking about silence is: when does silence really happen because no one has anything to say, and when does it happen because people are thinking about they want to say or are too intimidated to speak? It takes different people different lengths of time to realize when the floor is open and they can speak.

Before I learned that silence was a good thing, I just started speaking if no one else was talking and I had a thought complete enough to share; other people wait an extra second or two just to make sure they aren't stepping on anyone in the conversation. If you have a person who is always filling the silence, the more "polite" communicators will never have a chance to have *their* voices heard.

As you create your team's communication fingerprint, think about how silence can be allowed. I am not saying you have to mandate a certain length of time for a pause between each speaker—that would make for a very stilted conversation. As a team, just talk about it. How do you work "think time" into a conversation?

If you have someone on the team who fills silence, either by repeating their point or saying 'uhhhhh' or 'ummm' while they think so they don't lose the floor, talk to them about it. I know someone who says, "What else can I tell you...?" trailing off at the end. It makes it clear to me, as a listener, that she is not finished speaking and I should not start. That isn't true silence.

For coaches or captains who are leading meetings, silences can feel a lot longer than they really are. If you ask a question and no one jumps in right away with an answer, you might be tempted to further explain your point or move on assuming everyone agrees.

Try counting to ten and then saying something like, "Are there no thoughts on that?" or "Was the question clear?" to check if the team is ready to move on to the next point or if they are thinking about their response.

It might also be helpful to ask for understanding in a different way. Rather than saying, "Does anyone have any questions?" which requires someone to admit they don't understand and voice a question about it, ask "Did I explain that clearly?" or "Does everyone feel like they understand?" then look for nodding heads. If you don't see people nodding, it is likely they didn't really understand.

You can follow up with, "I am feeling like maybe I didn't make that as clear as I could have. Can we have a conversation about it, just for my personal wellbeing?" At that point, you can check for understanding and the team will feel less intimidated.

Observe how your team handles silence. How does silence make you feel? Do you have someone in your group who is always filling the space with words or sounds? Is the only time you get to think about a conversation *after* it is over? If you often think about what you should have said or a point you wish you had made after the opportunity has passed, your meetings likely don't have enough silence in them. Your team will communicate better if you talk about creating pauses to think during meetings; it will get you one step closer to being able to maintain conversations effectively and be your most productive.

The Golden Rule is Failing Us!

From the time we are very young, we are taught to treat others the way we would like others to treat us. It is the simple catch-all rule about playing nice, being kind, helping each other, and thinking about the other person's feelings. On the surface it seems like a very valid point: if we treat people the way we want them to treat us, all will be wonderful and life will be happy, right? I hate to be the bearer of bad news but, no, that isn't how it works.

* * *

My very best friend, whom I would trust with my life without hesitation, called me one morning and in a very solemn voice said, "I have something I need to tell you." Of course my response was that she could tell me anything.

She proceeded to tell me her brother had just told the family he was gay and that her parents were not taking it well. We talked at length about the challenges of the situation and how we could best be supportive to her brother and to help her parents. It was an emotionally intense conversation for me.

After we hung up, I continued to think about her brother and how this might affect her family. Five minutes later she called me back and, laughing hysterically, said, "April Fool's! I was just pulling your leg! He's not gay!"

I was completely devastated. I do not like practical jokes. I certainly do not like to be made fool of and I did not believe the emotionally charged subject of someone's sexuality should be a topic of fodder for April Fool's Day.

After what seemed like forever, she stopped laughing and said, "Oh, come on, lighten up. It's just a joke." To which I responded, "If I trust you enough that you could pull such a stunt, I would expect you to respect me enough not to" and hung up the phone.

* * *

The friend in that story believed practical jokes to be funny and good-natured. No doubt her other friends pulled them on each other regularly to the delight of everyone involved. However, in treating me that way, grave damage was done to the friendship because I felt lied to and emotionally abused. The golden rule most certainly did not apply.

A very similar problem arises with the word 'respect.' It seems like a pretty clear word. There are several definitions, but the one most people intend when they use it is: "to show regard or consideration for." Simple enough. But it's not actually that simple at all. In fact, it is quite challenging.

Being respectful can differ by culture. Should you look an authority figure in the eye, or not? Is telling the coach you don't understand her instructions something you can say on the field in front of other players, or not? If a player is taken out of the starting lineup and she cries, is she showing passion about the sport or is she questioning the coach's decision and being selfish?

Think back a couple of chapters to the team of athletes who voiced ongoing frustration because their coach was constantly accusing them of being disrespectful and had created a long list of behaviors they had to follow. The team walked on eggshells every time they interacted with her.

At the same time, the coach was disappointed that the athletes would not come and talk to her about any of their concerns or ideas for the team. She felt like she had to drag them into her office kicking and screaming to have simple conversations.

The team code of conduct had pages of rules about eating during meetings, expected eye contact during film review, the use of cell phones on the bus home from games, speaking when spoken to, what was the appropriate response to a text message from the coach, the number of hours allowed to respond to an email, and a list of times when crying was not allowed. I was shocked to see such a regimen of expected respect in writing. No wonder the team was afraid. *I* was intimidated and I didn't even have to follow all those rules!

The issue was that the coach had a very specific set of ideas about how she showed respect for authority and it worked best for her when expectations where listed clearly as 'rules' to follow. Couple that with her own feelings of insecurity in her role as head coach. She was essentially saying, "I want you to respect me," but when she did not get the results she expected, she became almost tyrannical in her list of directives.

In contrast, once she believed she had the talent, skill, and knowledge to be a head coach and realized her team was showing her respect, she no longer needed the list of behaviors and punitive results for failing to meet them in order to *feel* respected and in control.

So, instead of treating people in the way that would work best for *you* and expecting them to respond how *you* would, figure out what you want the end result to be and how *they* want to be treated to get there.

Sit down and talk to your teammates about how you achieve that result *together*. It is amazing how creative people can be when they work together toward a goal without having a specific path on how to get there laid out for them. The Golden Rule is only one, narrow path towards valuing and appreciating each other, and it forgets how unique each one of us is.

Creating Personal Boundaries

Why is telling people the truth about how we feel and what we want so difficult? How many times have you walked away from a conversation thinking, "How did I get talked into *that*?" Have you ever gone along with something just because you didn't want to cause waves, even though you knew you were going to end up in a place you didn't really want to be? It happens to the best of us. And once you've agreed to something, it is twice as hard to go back and un-agree. So, you decide to just do whatever it is to keep the peace, even though you really don't want to. Every time that happens, your personal boundaries are being breached and a little bit of you is being taken away.

So, how can we create boundaries and take care of ourselves, yet not feel like we are being mean? Here are a few ideas to consider so the next time you need to say "no" you'll have the tools to do so in a way that is heard and respected:

> ***Believe that you are important and that you matter.*** Doing someone a favor is great, and I am a huge proponent of going out of your way for others—just not at the expense of taking care of yourself. Check in with yourself and make sure your needs are being met before other people's favors. Going along with the crowd just because you want to fit in is not respecting yourself as a strong, important individual.

You don't have to explain why. When someone asks you why you won't do something, they are looking for reasons they can explain away or downgrade so they can get what they want. Don't try to justify your boundary when they push it. Keep repeating that you are unable or don't want to do what they are asking. "It doesn't work for me," "I'm not interested," and "I don't want to" are perfectly acceptable answers.

Being blindsided will get you every time. When that little voice in your head is jumping up and down screaming, trying to get your attention, it means you need a chance to think about what you are being asked before you answer. Try listening to yourself. These statements will give you some space to think: "I need a bit to process that;" "Can I get back to you tomorrow?"; "I really want to jump right in and say 'yes,' but I've learned that I need to check my schedule before adding something new;" "I would really hate for you to be counting on me and have to back out;" "I'll call you back this afternoon;" "I'm not feeling very comfortable with that, so I'm going to have to say 'no, thanks'."

Call it like it is. When you have to tell someone 'no,' sometimes it works best if you let them know you are setting a personal boundary. Acknowledge the request—"I can really tell you need some help on this"—then set your boundary: "In this case, I need to create some boundaries around my [work, family, personal time, etc.] and I'm not going to be able to do that for you."

Let your 'no' be 'no.' If you say 'no' and use the creating-boundaries reason, you absolutely cannot let someone badger you into changing your answer to a 'yes.' If you give in once, you will teach people that your 'no' does not actually mean 'no,' but really means they have to push, nag, and pressure you. If something in your schedule changes and you can change your mind, fine—

explain it that way, and by all means help out. But boundaries only work if you actually keep them once you set them.

Respect the boundaries of others. Part of being able to set personal boundaries is accepting when others do so. You might not like it; you might wish it was different but sometimes even the people we love have to take care of themselves first. And that is okay. In fact not only is it okay, it is healthy.

Maintaining healthy personal boundaries helps teammates know where they stand with each other. When personal boundaries are not clear, misunderstandings can arise. Eliminate the risk of the frustration that comes from feeling taken advantage of by helping every member of your team establish and understand where her own personal boundaries are. Boundaries are easier to defend if you know where they are *before* you need them.

* * *

I used to play pickup beach volleyball every weekend with a group of friends. After playing all day we would toss something on the grill and enjoy each other's company. It was not uncommon for the blender to being going with various flavors of margaritas and one person would walk around topping off glasses.

One Saturday night, Tony was filling glasses. People would protest, but he would fill their glass anyway. When he got to me, he looked at me and, without saying a word, I waved him off. He moved on to the next glass.

Al was sitting next to me and protested, "Wait a minute! I tell you 'no more' and you fill my glass anyway. She just waves her hand and you pass her by. What's up with that?"

Tony replied, "When you say 'no' and I fill your glass, you drink it. When *she* says 'no' and I fill her glass, she leaves it sitting there and it gets wasted."

I learned that night that having my actions match my words made it almost unnecessary to defend my boundaries because people didn't push them.

* * *

The Truth Shouldn't Hurt

"I just wish someone had told me. I feel like such a fool. It seems like everyone knew but me."

I quietly listened as the junior star athlete and 'A' student continued to lament:

"We've been together since senior year (of high school). We talked about marriage, kids, where we wanted to live...." Her voice trailed off.

I was surprised she wasn't crying. Maybe she was still in shock. For the moment, she seemed angrier that no one had had the guts to tell her than that her four-year relationship had come to an abrupt and messy end.

"He has a *kid*! I mean *really*? My mom saw him walking with the girl, pushing a stroller, and she let him talk his way out of it. It's a small town, for Pete's sake! Everyone knows everyone else's business and nobody could be bothered to pick up the phone and let me know he has this whole other life going on while I'm away at school?"

* * *

How many times have you heard (or maybe said) "the truth hurts"? That phrase seems to be a catch-all that claims, "I can say anything I want, any way that I want, without care or thought, as long as it is the truth." I disagree completely.

Sometimes we all need—and even *want*—to be told a painful or embarrassing truth. "There is spinach in your teeth." "The internship you wanted went to someone else." "You are not going to start this week." How that information is delivered can make the difference between it being very painful or being just a little sting. Some of that difference lies in the intent, some in the delivery, and some in the message itself. To keep hurt to a minimum, consider the following:

> ***Just because something is true, does not mean it needs to be said.*** "That baby is ugly." That might be true. Some babies look a little squished for a few days after they're born, but there is absolutely no excuse for saying something like that. Consider the "truth" you want to tell—does it really need to be said?
>
> ***What is there to gain from this truth?*** If the only benefit to a truth being spoken is to make the speaker feel better, it should not be said. Hurting someone else for your benefit is just plain mean. In describing a friend, I once said, "She is a bleach blonde." It was true. But it was also hurtful and unnecessary; I should not have said it. In contrast, some truths need to be told, even if the person can't, or won't, acknowledge it right then, because there is so much to lose if the truth stays hidden. Cheating boyfriends, drinking or drug problems, and making major life mistakes fall into that category.
>
> ***Are you the right person to tell this truth?*** Even if your intent is not malicious and someone could benefit from hearing the truth, you might not be the right person to say it. On the other hand, using the excuse that you are not the right person simply because

the truth is difficult or 'messy' to tell is not right, nor fair, to anyone. Be honest about what needs to be said and what your role should be.

So, you've determined the truth needs to be said, the hearer will benefit from it, and you are the right person to tell them. *Now what?*

No one wants to be told a painful truth in front of other people. Take the person aside and speak to them in private. Being able to react to the discomfort of a hard truth without the embarrassment of being observed by others will go a long way to limiting the hurt.

Provide an intro. Never just blurt out a hurtful truth. Start by saying something like, "I have something I need to share with you and I'm uncomfortable about it," then take a breath. It will give the hearer a moment to prepare herself.

Know what you want to say and get to the point. If you are going to tell someone a painful truth, get to it already; don't beat around the bush or change your mind. It is like taking off a bandage, quicker is better.

Let the person express their hurt. If you are a big enough person to tell someone a painful truth, be big enough to stay in the conversation and let them work through their reaction to it.

Meet the person where they are. Sometimes it is appropriate to help someone develop ideas for solutions or fixes to the 'truth' you just shared. If you can be helpful, do so. If they aren't ready to problem-solve, just listen.

Keep the discussion to yourself. A painful truth someone needed to hear should never be used as fodder for the amusement of others. If you can't keep the conversation to yourself, don't have it.

Telling someone the truth—a real, honest, painful truth—is hard. It can also be one of the greatest signs of true friendship, caring, and love. That is why I so often say, "love each other enough to give tough feedback (tell the truth); trust each other enough to apply it."

Making Others Feel Heard

The ability to listen is a critical component to effective communication. However, *listening is different than understanding* and *understanding is different than making someone feel heard*. When I was a teenager, I had siblings who were toddlers. Very often when I asked them to do something, they would simply ignore me and continue doing what they wanted to do instead. The conversation that followed sounded like this:

Me: "You need to listen to me."

Sibling: "I *am!*"

Me: "No, you amn't!" (my made-up contraction for 'am' and 'not')

That interaction is an example of them listening and understanding, but me not feeling heard. Certainly my sibling heard me. No doubt they understood what I wanted them to do. They simply did not want to do it. I would tell them they weren't listening, when what I wanted was for them to *act* on what I was saying, not just hear it.

* * *

When someone doesn't do what we suggest or doesn't act on our ideas, we feel like they aren't listening. In actuality, they probably heard us just fine. The issue is either they didn't understand or they considered our advice and decided to do something different. We have no way of knowing which it is, so we end up feeling like we weren't heard and figure it isn't worth our trouble to try to give that person information in the future. That is a really bad situation if you were the listener, because a path of communication has been shut down.

As coaches and team members, we know that productive communication is key to our success—the last thing we want to do is squelch the flow of information. So how do we convey that not only are we *listening* but we also *understand*, even if we make a decision that goes against what was said? We have to actively engage in the conversation.

Active listening is the label placed on the behaviors that lead to someone feeling heard. Actually doing it can feel fake at first, but once you get used to it, you will find it really does reduce miscommunication and the speaker will go away from the conversation feeling heard.

Here are a few tips to help you and your team get started:

> ***Prepare yourself to listen.*** Avoid jumping to conclusions, becoming defensive, and all the other things we talked about in Don't Shoot the Messenger. This means managing your internal emotional response and being open to what is being said.
>
> ***Check for understanding throughout the conversation.*** Use sentences like, "Let me make sure I understand...." "What I think you are saying is..." "If I understood you correctly..." "It sounds like you are frustrated by..." If your understanding is not quite in line with what the person is trying to tell you, give them a chance to restate themselves.
>
> ***Put a label on the feeling you believe the person is trying to communicate*** (use the *Feelings Words List* if you would like). This

will allow you to show understanding or permit the speaker to explain it in a different way, if needed.

Remember that feeling heard requires verbal and nonverbal acknowledgement. Look at the person talking to you and encourage them to talk. Pay attention to what is being conveyed and respond with nods, a quizzical look, or say "hmm, I understand." Ignore the ringing phone or the 'ding' of your email.

Be careful not to judge the information as good or bad. Doing so is likely to make the speaker feel like you are judging her personally and that will shut her down. If you aren't clear about what is being said, ask the speaker to say more. Don't make up a 'why' for her. Ask her to tell you why she is feeling the way she is (remember, you can't observe why).

Once she has finished speaking, ***summarize the suggestion or the information to verify you are on the same page and thank her***. "I will have to put some thought into that." "That idea may have some merit." "I will add that to our list of options." "Thanks, I appreciate it." And mean it. Nothing will cause you to lose the confidence of your teammates faster than being perceived as a fake.

Finally, and this is important, ***follow up and let the person know how you used the information they provided.*** If you decided to go in a different direction, explain that you took what they said into account and provide a brief explanation as to why you chose an alternative path. Remember, they can't observe why you made the decision you did, and they will make something up if you don't tell them.

I am not suggesting you have to go through this step-by-step process every time someone wants to speak to you. For the important conversations, absolutely—I recommend using all of the steps. For simpler interactions, just being aware of the steps and realizing it is important to make others feel heard might be enough. Try it in simple conversations with people you trust, who can help you practice. It will make a big difference on your team and in your personal life when people feel like you are listening to understand, not just to hear.

Creating a Safe Environment

You're doing all the right things: you don't shoot the messenger; you understand that you can't observe 'why'; you ask questions; and you make sure people feel heard when they talk to you. Still, the information you need to know is not getting to you—your team seems to be afraid to talk. So what's the deal?

It is important to realize that most of us have learned not to be very trusting of other people (remember the tiger behind every tree). When someone says, "I have an open-door policy; you can talk to me anytime about anything," we somehow know that anything we say can, and will, be used against us. If you are trying to change that perception, it is going to take a while and you will have to be very consistent. If someone is brave enough to speak up, reward that behavior.

There are other reasons athletes don't want to talk to their coaches or captains: sometimes teams have a strong 'us versus them' mentality between leaders and 'regular' players. That boundary can be daunting. If there are emotional leaders on your team who don't believe it is safe to talk to you, they can make the whole team believe it isn't safe.

Figure out who those leaders are and talk to them. For heaven's sake, do not accuse them of anything (that would be proving them right that it's not safe to talk to you). Ask them how you can work together to make the team great. Ask them to provide feedback about how the team perceives you. Show them that you are able to hear constructive information and use it to make changes.

Once you can get those leaders on your side, they will take positive news back to the team. Soon enough, others will become brave and start sharing their ideas. If you have an emotional leader who is toxic, you have a different problem on your hands (see Chapter Eight, dealing with toxic people).

Sometimes the boundary that keeps people from feeling safe is a physical one. Do you have an office with four walls and a door? Even if the door is always standing open, people must walk into your space to talk to you. If your schedule is always so full that they have to make an appointment to see you, it is even *less* likely they will talk openly with you.

Make yourself available. Walk around, talk to your team, and get to know them as people. Put everyone's name in a hat and randomly pick out people to invite to lunch in small groups. The more accessible you are, the easier it will be for your team to share difficult or important things with you.

When you have team meetings, do you always sit at the head of the table or at the front of the room and run the meeting? If so, your team will look to you to supply all the answers rather than being creative and coming up with solutions on their own. Consider sitting along the side of the table and having someone else run the meeting. If it is an option, get rid of the table altogether and just sit in a circle.

When I work with athletes, is it not uncommon for me to sit on the floor with them. If you can make yourself physically 'one of them,' your team will be more likely to accept you and open up to you. And don't worry—your authority and their respect will not be tarnished.

Another possibility is to give people the option to share their ideas anonymously. Put up a suggestion box or an envelope where they can leave thoughts and ideas; whatever works for your team. If the team is concerned about their handwriting being recognized, have them type and print their submissions. When you get a useful suggestion, make a big deal about it. Talk about it in meetings and make changes based on it. You want to do everything in your power to make the person who submitted that suggestion *want* to take credit for it.

When you get an idea that you *can't* implement, bring it up in a meeting and talk about why it isn't practical right now. But say you are thankful for the idea and that you will keep it in mind. Those are small steps toward your team being willing to share things with you directly.

Never let an idea fall through the cracks. If someone takes the time to share something and they never hear anything else about it, they will assume it was never read or considered. When that information gets back to the team, it will further cement their thoughts about you being inaccessible, and you will hear even less from them. Once you prove that you're willing to listen without judgment, you will be surprised how quickly your team becomes willing to share good news, bad news, issues, concerns, and ideas with you.

* * *

The coach sat smugly behind his desk. "I told you they were happy with my plan," he said.

I frowned. I knew the team didn't like his plan at all. My response was measured, "Oh? Why do you say that?"

"I asked them in the team meeting today if anyone had any objections, and no one said anything. I even told them if they didn't want to speak up in the group that they could come to my office and talk to me in private. No one showed up."

It was all I could do to keep from rolling my eyes. *Of course* no one said anything or came to his office—he would badger and intimidate *me* if he disagreed with something I said; I could only imagine how he treated the athletes when *they* tried to talk to him. His office door was always closed. If they showed up without an appointment, they never knew how long they would have to wait to see him. And he didn't really use their ideas anyway. How he translated that into them being "happy" was beyond me.

MY COMMUNICATION PLAYBOOK

Chapter Eight
Productive Conflict Will Save You

All the problems of the world are caused by people who do not listen.
–Franco Zeffirelli, quoted in *The Observer,* 1998

When a conversation starts to head downhill, don't go down with it.
–Doc Robyn

Reprove a friend in secret, but praise (her) before others.
–Leonardo Da Vinci

* * *

Having Tough Conversations

I looked in shock at the email I had received from the head coach. I read it again, just to make sure I wasn't missing something. The tone was so nasty! He had never spoken to me like that and I certainly had not given him any reason to start doing so now. It seemed he was blaming me for "his" team missing a spin class which was scheduled after their meeting with me that week.

I was confused. My meeting with the team earlier in the week had involved a difficult discussion. I had felt it was important that I stay and see it through to the end. When the team asked me to extend my time with them, I specifically asked if they had anything else scheduled after our meeting. They had told me their schedule was open. So why was I getting an email attacking me for "making a unilateral decision that *my* work was more important than the spin instructor's?"

I was going to have to have a heart-to-heart conversation with the team. Either there had been a misunderstanding about scheduling or they had lied to me. In either case, the email I had received was not an acceptable way to communicate a concern. I was going to have to bring that up with the coach. Suddenly I was not looking forward to meeting with them the following week.

* * *

Nobody enjoys having difficult conversations. Consider the teammate who leaves her practice gear in her locker until the air is so thick with the stench you can *see* it; the roommate who says, "I'll pay for the pizza next time" but never does; the group member who just isn't pulling her weight on a class project; the athlete you really like as a person but are going to have to cut from the team.

Yeah, *those* conversations. Nobody likes them. It is one reason gossip happens. It is much easier to complain to someone else than address the problem directly. It may be easier, but it doesn't solve anything; in fact it will make things *worse*.

If your team has developed a communication fingerprint, you already have an accepted method for addressing these types of conflict while they are still small annoyances. If you don't have one, your job is going to be a little more challenging—not impossible, just a bit challenging. The following steps will put you on the path toward having a successful conversation:

Step 1: Make sure you know exactly what is bothering you and what the best solution is for you. Be prepared to compromise, but you must know going in what it is that you would like so you'll know what to say.

Step 2: Don't ambush the person. Nobody wants to be called out in a public setting or without time to prepare. You have been thinking about this issue and this conversation for a long time; they have been going through life happy-go-lucky thinking (or at least pretending) that everything is fine. Have an idea of a private place you can talk. Begin with a statement like, "I have a concern I'd like to talk to you about. Is now a good time or can we schedule something later today?"

Step 3: Own your part of the concern by starting the conversation with an "I" statement. For example: "Joan, I really don't mind covering for you on pizza night now and then. Maybe it slipped your mind, but I really need you to pay me back." "Marcy, I've noticed that you will sometimes start bouncing the ball on your knee when Coach is talking and I get distracted. I'm sure you do it unconsciously, so I was wondering if you could help me come up with an inconspicuous way I could point it out to you," or "For us to be successful on this group project, we all need to do our part. How can I help you get your section completed?" Be careful about conveying blame.

Step 4: Actively listen. Give the person space to talk and/or explain. Engage in a conversation with them to make sure you understand and they feel heard (see Chapter Seven, *Making Others Feel Heard*).

Step 5: Be gracious and keep your cool while sticking to your need for change. If you let your emotions take over, the conversation will only make things worse. If the person becomes defensive, roll with it. "I can understand that you would be upset. It's an awkward conversation for me, too. I just felt it was better for us to talk about it now rather than for me to just stew until I couldn't take it anymore."

Step 6: Pay attention to your internal dialogue. Is the conversation sticking with the subject or is the person talking about everything *except* the subject at hand? Guide them back to the topic you are trying to discuss. If they bring up something else that is bothering them, promise to discuss that issue when you finish the current one.

Step 7: Reach an understanding. The point of the conversation is for you to understand them and for them to understand you. Work a solution together. Once you reach it, make sure each of you knows what success looks like. If an apology is in order, offer or accept it graciously.

Step 8: When you notice positive change, be genuinely thankful as appropriate. Many people like to have positive things pointed out in public, but if it will embarrass them, pull them aside and acknowledge that you have noticed their efforts. If they are trying to improve and feel that no one is noticing, they will feel like they are wasting their time and go back to their old ways.

Some people find it useful to practice tough conversations *before* they have them in order to work through the vocabulary and deal with the stressful feelings. Ask someone you trust to help you, then make sure you are actually practicing the conversation, *not* gossiping about the situation. If you don't have anyone to talk it through with you, make sure you do a thorough job of Step One.

Remember, it is always better to have the conversation as soon as you have your talking points clear in your head. The discomfort you feel will only get worse the longer you wait.

When a Conversation Spins Out of Control

"You make me so angry! You are thoughtless and stupid and I regret ever trying to be friends with you!"

The girl being attacked looked shell-shocked. Granted, she had promised to drive her teammate to practice and in her rush that morning had forgotten—an egregious lapse, to be sure. But screaming that her teammate was thoughtless and stupid in front of the team and coaches? Regretting a *three-year* friendship? *Really*?

* * *

It is easy to become emotionally hooked into a situation. The ability to have a rational, controlled conversation can evaporate when stress hormones start coursing through our bodies. Things are said to hurt the other person. Words are used to slice and dice our opponent, even if she is a friend. Friendships which have taken years to cultivate, die in an instant at the hand of an emotionally charged argument. There are tears of regret when the realization dawns that a friendship has been permanently damaged by careless words spoken in anger. Teams are torn apart by the toxic spewing of emotion.

Unfortunately, this type of drama is not a rare occurrence. I have no doubt that you can think of stories just like this one from your own team. The emotional scars that result can last a lifetime.

The good news is that teams can learn healthier, more productive ways to handle disagreements and conflict—to be able to address the problem, develop a solution, and move past it, no matter how big a crisis it is. There are three stages to any conflict: the beginning or *trigger;* the middle, where the communication and *internal dialogue* take place; and, finally, the *result*. If you can recognize the trigger and manage the conversation by observing your internal dialogue, you will have control over the result.

Catching the trigger point

The first step to managing any situation is recognizing that it needs to be managed. You have to catch the *trigger point*. The trigger is the moment a conversation goes from being just a conversation to being a possible confrontation or 'incident.' The trigger of a confrontation can be tough to notice when it is actually happening. After a major argument—when the participants are trying to pick up the damaged feelings and bruised egos—the trigger, or point of no return, can often be identified easily.

Identifying the trigger in hindsight can result in a productive learning experience, if used by a team to understand the process of conversation maintenance. The ultimate goal is to be able to detect the feelings before and during the moment of trigger in order to make decisions that will change the course and outcome of the conversation.

The emotions and feelings that occur during the escalation of a conversation or argument are often overlooked in the heat of a rising battle. Many people believe feelings are not logical and, therefore, not important—but that is a major mistake. Feelings are what drive decisions. When the intensity of a conversation starts to rise, emotions are what get out of control and cause us to say or do things we later regret. Since they are so important and often overlooked, it is important to take time to think about what emotions feel like on a physical level.

The process

Think about what it feels like (physically) when you become frustrated or angry—most people find it helpful to write it down. I am not talking about words like 'angry' or 'mad' or other words from the feelings word list—instead, think about the actual physical response your body has to a situation when you are about to enter into a verbal struggle. What is your fight or flight response? Some common answers include: chest tightness; flushing; accelerated heart rate; feeling hot; short, quick breathing; and feeling tension in your back or shoulders.

Go ahead and think about yours. The last time you were in a heated discussion with someone, what did it feel like? Write it down. It is an important piece to the puzzle for being able to catch a trigger point and manage a conversation in the direction you want it to go.

Okay, now you know what it feels like when something is aggravating you. Make a mental note to take notice the next time you have feelings like that. Could it be a trigger to a situation? Are you involved or just observing other people in a confrontation? At first, making this type of observation as it happens is going to be really hard. You will realize after the fact and think, "darn, I missed it," but don't get discouraged—you'll improve with practice.

Next time you might be able to identify the trigger just moments after it happened or as it is happening. Eventually, you will start to feel your physical response to annoyance when it starts, and be able to take a step back to think, "hold on a minute; I am starting to feel angry. What is going on here, and how do I want to handle it?" That is when you know you are in control. You no longer have to allow a rollercoaster of emotions to dictate how your conversations go. You can make logical, cool-headed decisions based on your feelings, rather than your feelings deciding things for you which you'll regret later.

Conversation management

Now that you have the ability to tap into your body's early-warning system for conflict, what do you do with that information? You know conversations can quickly spiral out of control, and you have to make decisions in very short order to keep it from happening. Your self-observation isn't over; in fact, it has just started. Throughout the conversation, you need to stay checked into your feelings. Are they continuing to escalate, staying the same, or calming?

All of this information is valuable data—and not only for you; the other person in the conversation would benefit greatly if she also understood how you are feeling. Managing a conversation means being able to recognize, manage, and articulate your internal dialogue, which is made up of responses to the emotions you are feeling. You are going to need to be able to share those feelings. Use the skills you learned in Chapter Seven and the *Feeling Words List* to put your internal dialogue into words. Let the other person know what is going on in your head.

The result

The result of a conversation is the make-it-or-break-it point. Did you end up in a good place or a bad place? Were you able to steer the discussion where you wanted it to go, or did it run away with you? Is the situation resolved, on hold, hidden under a veil of 'nice'? Maybe it isn't over at all; maybe there is resentment or open contempt. If the answer is anything other than 'resolved' or 'mutually on hold until a specified time,' you have work to do.

As you get better at conversation maintenance, more and more of your interactions will result in solutions or agreement for further discussion and fewer will have negative outcomes followed by regret. It isn't easy, but you and your team can learn to do it. If you want to be a champion at communication, it takes dedication and practice just like a technical skill you practice to become a champion athlete.

Put an End to Gossip

My boyfriend called and asked if he could pick me up for lunch—a nice surprise, since he very rarely had time for lunch. As I got in the car, he handed me a single red rose (how sweet), I gave him a quick kiss, and we headed out to find something to eat.

None of that is interesting or even noteworthy. However, by the time I got back about an hour later, one of my teammates (who had been outside when I left) had told several people that I was cheating on my boyfriend. She had never met my boyfriend; she had no idea who he was, or who the guy was who had picked me up. She had decided that he could not have been my boyfriend because he brought me flowers. Apparently she didn't think guys did that for girls they were already dating.

The story became a huge firestorm, with hotspots flaring up constantly. Some people defended me while others argued that it must be true because I "looked like" the type of girl who would cheat. Starting that day, and for the entire two years I had remaining on that team, I defended myself. "Yes, the man who had taken me to lunch was my boyfriend and, yes, sometimes he even brings me flowers."

* * *

Why did my going to lunch with someone (my boyfriend or otherwise) really matter to anyone? That lunch date, the person I was with, or anything else about my personal life in no way changed my ability to do my job and do it well.

As part of an athletic team, you certainly have first-hand stories like that one. Maybe it was about you; maybe it is something you heard about someone else. But they happen all the time, and they are bad for team cohesiveness, trust, and performance. Trust is a key ingredient for a team to be successful. Without it, team members never join together like a well-oiled machine and perform to their potential. After that incident, I never trusted that teammate; it directly affected our ability to work together and to accomplish as much as we could have as a team.

Here are a few tips to keep things that have nothing to do with the goals of your team from turning into a firestorm fueled by gossip:

Open a discussion with your teammates about the damaging effects of gossip. Everyone will agree it is bad and no one in the room will stand up and say they think talking behind someone's back is a good thing. Let them tell stories about gossip they have heard, the hurt it caused, and how they have seen it harm teams in the past. You want the team to join together in sharing the negative experiences they have had with gossip.

Get a commitment that, as a team, you are going to wipe out gossip and the firestorm it creates. You might even want to include an agreement about gossip in your code of conduct (see Section Three for a team contract you can use as a guide). Some teams have even posted it on their locker room wall and signed the wall. If you don't want to have a signed piece of paper, create an explicit verbal agreement.

Have everyone agree to hold each other accountable to the agreement. Gossip cannot happen when no one is listening. Create phrases that can be used to easily remind someone about the team agreement (see Chapter Seven, creating a team vocabulary). "That sounds like an issue between you and Sue. Have you talked to her?" "I'm not really sure what happened between Meg and Dave, but I think it is their issue to work out." "I would be happy to help you prepare for the conversation it sounds like you need to have with Coach." Having something ready-made to say will make the uncomfortable situation of turning off gossip much easier.

Tell new team members about your "No-Gossip" policy. Explain why you put it in place, and if you have a written statement, share it with them. Make it clear that team drama has no place on your team.

Keep in mind that gossip and politics are very normal in group environments. It will take effort to change the team's behavior—but it is well worth the productive outcome you will receive. As long as everyone is committed to making it work, it will work!

Finally, ***coaches and captains, be role models***—this is a must. I cannot even count the number of times I have sat in meetings with a coach or player who complains bitterly about team drama and then it turned out they are the worst gossip on the team. Don't let that happen to you!

It really is this simple. Gossip and team drama will eat your team from the inside out if you don't talk about how your team handles them. You will waste valuable time and energy on things that impact your ability to win—just as much as whether or not I was having lunch with my boyfriend impacted my ability to work—and it will drain your resources. So ask yourself this question: *How much potential are you willing to waste on gossip and drama?*

Address an Existing Problem

It was pre-season—a time when athletes typically love catching up with old teammates and getting to meet the incoming newbies. As a fall sport, the pre-season started before the dorms were open, so the whole team spent the first week or two living in a local hotel. It was a great time for the team to begin to gel and figure out how the new pieces fit with the old. But this year was different—this team had a lot of baggage left over from the previous spring.

I spent two hours sitting on a hotel dresser with 25 college women stretched out on the beds, floor, and chairs around me. The freshmen looked confused as the older members of the team talked over each other in an effort to recount why the team was so angry.

"It was like they were setting a trap for us!"

"They only told *one* member of the team we weren't allowed to have a party!"

"It was her 21st birthday and it met the rules in our code of conduct! If they expected us not to have a party, they should have told the *whole* team, not just one person, *hoping* that we would all figure it out!"

"That's not the worst of it! The worst part is they parked their car outside the apartment and just waited! They were *stalking* us!"

"The next day, they (the coaches) called a team meeting and started asking who attended the 'forbidden' party, then called out people they had seen there. Anyone who admitted to being there, or who someone could 'prove' was there, was punished. There were a lot of people who didn't admit it and they got off scot-free. That is totally *not* cool."

This team did not have a communication fingerprint or any other method for handling conflict. The "they" who were in the car were two of the assistant coaches. It seemed the head coach had approved, or at least looked the other way regarding, the late-night stakeout. But the not-so-undercover surveillance of the birthday party was only the tip of the iceberg. The clash between the coaching staff and the athletes was tearing the team apart, and the hurt feelings of some athletes being punished while others lied about being at the party had created festering bitterness. Star players were looking to transfer; athletes were in the Athletic Director's office complaining on an almost-weekly basis; the head coach was losing control of her team. Her job was going to be in jeopardy if something wasn't done, and done quickly.

* * *

When a team has this much pent-up energy and drama, the first thing they need to do is vent—but not the kind of venting that escalates emotions and causes the tension to go from palpable to frenzied. When a team is retelling a frustrating story and there isn't someone to help keep the emotions under control, players can feed on each other's anger and feelings get worse instead of better.

The point of 'venting' is to release pressure—to allow the emotion to play itself out. In order for that to happen, it is very important that there be a facilitator who is not going to get hooked into the problem—someone who can stay objective and manage the energy in the room. Assuming you have someone to do that, here are the steps to resolving an existing issue on your team:

> ***Meet with the whole team.*** You might be tempted to bring in only the players you think were involved in the problem, or who were on the team when the situation occurred, but that would be a mistake. When a problem dates back to a previous season or to a particular large-scale event, firestorming amongst the team and with other athletes will balloon the situation into something much bigger than just the players who were directly involved. It is much better to bring everyone in, tell the story once for everyone to hear, and get them all on the same page. If you try to address just a subset of players, various perceptions of what happened in your meeting will leak out; players who were not invited will feel snubbed; and any progress you thought you made will be lost. So bring everybody: red shirts, injured, starters, depth chart, Freshmen through Seniors; sit them all down at once.
>
> ***Get the whole story.*** This might take some time. As players become more comfortable with the situation, they are going to want to start adding their piece to the puzzle—just make sure it is their piece. It is important that each player own her thoughts and

ideas by using "I" statements. Accounts of what happened and the feelings involved may start to overlap as players start to talk with each other about what happened, what they saw, and what they think took place. There might be disagreements. Be careful not to let anyone speak as if their side of the story were fact; everyone has an opinion of what happened, and that is what they are sharing, not facts. Let them sort through it. It is important that they talk until they reach a consensus about where the root of the problem lies. You will know when they get there—the same basic points will start to be repeated.

Summarize and get agreement. Once you have a grasp on what the main points are, summarize them and ask the team if what you just outlined indicates understanding of the whole picture. Give them an opportunity to clarify, add, or change details. Pay attention to everyone in the room. Do they look like they agree, or do they look like they still have stuff swirling in their head that needs to come out? It is important that everyone is on board—that the problem to be discussed is completely out in the open—or the process will fail.

Take a break. With major issues that involve an entire team, just the process of getting the problem out in the open can be exhausting and take hours. You don't have to try to also solve it in the same meeting. Take some time to sleep on it and recharge. Ending the meeting with a summary of what needs to be addressed (and everyone agreeing) will give you a specific place to start when you get together again.

Schedule the next meeting before you leave, if possible—the following day is best. Do not wait more than a couple of days or you will lose momentum and have to start again near the beginning. If you cannot schedule the time right then, make it clear that time will be scheduled very soon to continue working on the issue. Additionally, it is very important that everyone is in an emotionally comfortable place before anyone leaves. Check in with each team member; make eye contact and ask if they are in a good place to stop for now. If someone looks away, doesn't nod, or doesn't seem to be in a good place, ask them if they have something they need to bring up to the group or if they would like to talk to you in private.

Write it down. There is nothing worse than doing all that work and then having the details get fuzzy in your memory. Assign someone the task of typing up the major points (a simple bulleted list is fine) and emailing them to everyone. It can be the facilitator or a player; who fills the role doesn't matter, as long as it happens.

Come back together. When you get back together to continue the conversation, go over the bullet points and verify with the group that the list is complete and includes all of the issues that need to be addressed. Fill in any gaps and listen to concerns the team has. This session should not include a complete rehashing of the previous meeting's conversation—the goal is to summarize where you were, pick up where you left off, and continue to move toward resolution. Once everyone agrees that all the points are on the table, you are ready to start using productive conflict as it is outlined in Chapter Six.

The process of addressing a problem that a team has been firestorming about for a long time is the same as dealing with a new issue. However, old problems tend to come with more baggage, hurt feelings, and differences of opinion about what happened. Old issues will require more time to get the whole story on the table, brainstorming a solution will be more challenging, and hurt feelings and nursed grudges will take longer to heal. The underlying contempt and distrust that come from long-standing resentment will tear a team apart and keep them from performing to their potential. A team who recognizes this will be willing to commit to the effort and personal discomfort it takes to work through it.

If being a champion were easy, everyone would do it. Only those who are willing to give 100% to being the best they and their team can be will make it to the top—even when that means sitting down to talk through an interpersonal team conflict. Working through team issues can be more emotionally difficult than working hard at practice, but will give your team an edge beyond their physical ability to compete.

Toxic People Are Bad Apples

You're not alone. We've all had it happen: you start the day thinking life is pretty good, but after a run-in with Toxic Tammy you suddenly find yourself believing you might be the only intelligent being on the planet. Worse, that negative fungus spreads. Soon, everyone on your team is bemoaning how horrible things are and how there is no hope for change. Your team has a bad apple and she is draining your potential.

* * *

Bianca started complaining the moment she opened her car door: "Ugh! *Really*? We have to get up at six o'clock in the morning to go on a run? Why do we always have to run so *early*? Is there some scientific study that says early morning running will condition us better than running at a *reasonable* time? I *hate* this!"

The constant banter of negativity continued almost unabated for the entire eight-mile run. I think some of her teammates ran faster or slower just to get away from her.

* * *

Do you have a really talented athlete who is a cancer in the locker room? Or a member of your coaching staff who can drive the team to great success, but leaves the players emotionally damaged and broken? People like that are often tolerated because it is believed that the team is better *with* them than *without* them—but we often fail to take into account the price of the mental destruction they wreak on a team.

How much better could the team be (as a whole) if so much energy was not being expended to offset the bad apple? Toxic players are given power and leadership on a team because they are so physically talented. However, doing so gives them influence and authority to spread their negativity to the rest of the team. But not all is lost—you do not have to allow Cynical Sally to trash your team morale. You *do* have options.

You could cut the player, but then you lose the talent. You could keep her and expend lots of time and energy trying to deal with her venomous attitude every time it rears its ugly head. Or you can inoculate your team against it, while working with her to improve her attitude and understanding of the positive role she could play. *That* is a win all the way around—you get to keep the talented player, the team learns not to give her the power to be toxic, and she might even learn to be a *positive* leader.

Here is a quick look at what you can and cannot control as far as team toxicity, and where you can make changes to inoculate yourself and your team against the spores of pessimism:

> ***Identify the source.*** This sounds like it should be simple; however, it is important to know if the person you are dealing with is really generating negativity, or if they are bent on spreading gloom-and-doom they pick up elsewhere. Someone who is passing along

negativity can be taught better coping skills; a truly negative person is more difficult to stop.

Determine specific behaviors the negative person engages in that are toxic to the team. Some examples might be: complaining during practice; practicing at half speed because she knows she is good enough to start without having to give 100% during the week; not keeping up with her academic or other responsibilities; or bad mouthing the coaching staff or other players. The list of possible negative behaviors is endless.

Take the time to determine exactly what behaviors need to change. Telling someone they have a bad attitude isn't going to give her the information she needs to change. What exactly are you observing that translates into "bad attitude"? What does a "bad attitude" look like?

Once you can recognize her unwanted behavior, ***make a list of behaviors you would like to see instead***. What does it look like to give 100% at practice? How can you tell she isn't giving her all, and how would you know if she did? What do you need to see academically to feel she is pulling her weight? What does a "good attitude" look like?

Now you know specifically what she is doing that you don't want, and you have an unambiguous list of behaviors you would like to see instead. Before you confront her with your lists, you need to ***think about what is motivating her to continue the existing behavior***. Are you implicitly rewarding bad behavior? What incentive is she receiving from the team to continue the unwanted behaviors?

Unfortunately, we often reward the exact behavior we wish would change. Some examples I have seen:

Letting a bad apple off easy at practice just so she will stop complaining and you can coach the rest of the team in peace;

Letting the team use one player's toxicity to get what they want: "We don't like that drill and if she complains enough about it, we won't have to do it";

Putting the toxic person in the starting lineup because you feel like you "need" her, even though she has blatantly broken a fundamental team rule. "What is Coach going to do, not play me? Pleeez, this team would lose without me and it's a contract year." *(Yes, I actually know of a player who said that out loud.)*

When the rules don't apply to your star players as they do to the rest of the team, other players will try to see how far *they* can bend the rules. The result is having no authority to enforce *any* of the team rules. Additionally, having a player who is above the rules gives her power—and giving a toxic person power allows them to take over the team.

Take an honest look at yourself, the coaching staff, and the team; if you find situations where you are reinforcing bad behavior, change it. There are likely to be complaints—no one likes it when they have been getting away with breaking the rules and the situation suddenly changes. But trust me—if *you* don't make a change, your toxic player will have no motivation to change. Here are some things to consider:

Provide motivation to make the wanted change. This is often a tough one. This is your star player; no doubt you feel like you can't sit her out of games as punishment for her behavior. I am not going to say whether you should or shouldn't; that is a decision that needs to be made on a case-by-case basis. But you *do* need to be creative: how can you push her to make needed changes? Is extra work at practice an option? Community service? Fines?

Think about what is important to this player. Maybe she really likes speaking to the press and being quoted in the paper—you can take that option away. Also consider if there are things you can use as rewards when she makes the changes you need to see. *Rewarding good behavior is often more productive than punishing bad behavior*—doing a combination of both will certainly help her be more motivated to change.

Don't hand out rewards just to get her up to 'acceptable' behavior—doing so will be un-motivating to the rest of the team. As an example: I had a boss who gave a coworker a monetary bonus to encourage him to come in on time and bring his output up to the department standard. As one of the top performers on the team, I quickly learned that slack behavior was rewarded and hard work was ignored. That is exactly *not* the standard you want to establish!

Ask your bad apple for solution ideas. This is where the rubber meets the road, so to speak. If you really have a Negative Nancy or a Miserable Maxine on your hands, you are going to get more of "woe is me, there is nothing to be done" or a defensive attitude when you start asking about ideas for solutions. If you have a team player who has not been feeling heard (and therefore keeps repeating the same negative stuff and bemoaning the lack of a solution), she will jump at the chance to develop a plan to make things better. If she has been so upset about it that she has been toxic, she has certainly thought about it enough to make helpful suggestions.

Take the person aside and talk. Sometimes the negative person doesn't realize the effect they are having on their teammates. Pointing it out and asking them to stop can be very effective. If they are really unaware of their detrimental attitude, agree upon a nonintrusive way to point it out. When I worked with a team who had this issue, they agreed on using the word "stress." When a member of the team started on a downward spiral, someone on the team would say, "You seem really *stressed* about that." This was a simple signal to indicate that the person was headed into toxicity. Provide specific examples of inappropriate behavior and what you need to see instead.

Be prepared to manage your emotions. Toxic people are often very skilled manipulators. If you lose your cool, she will have the upper hand. Let her rant and rave and carry on if need be, but stick to your need for change. Explain the negative affect her current behavior is having on the team and their ability to perform to their potential—use facts, not emotions. Make it clear that changes in her behavior are *expected* and how those changes will make the team better and more successful. Tap into her desire to be on a winning team and show her how change will make winning more likely because the team will not be wasting emotional energy dealing with her negativity.

Listen to her concerns. You might feel like you know all of her concerns already and no doubt there will be excuses and denials, but rather than listening to how bad she thinks things are, listen specifically to what she is complaining about. Is there anything that could be a legitimate issue that needs to be resolved? It is easy to write off everything she says as irrelevant or 'sour grapes,' but if your team has a nagging problem, you are going to hear it from the "town crier" first. Try to ignore the emotion and listen to the content. Is there something she is complaining about that the team actually needs to fix? Great! That is something you can work on.

Make her feel heard (see Chapter Seven on how to make others feel heard). Demonstrate to her that you understand how hard change can be. Let her know that you are willing to help motivate her to make a change. Share the ideas you have around motivation. Close the meeting by reemphasizing that change is *not* optional.

Enlist the rest of the team. A healthy team with a strong communication fingerprint will hold everyone on the team accountable to the same standard. If it is appropriate, hold a team meeting or ask your captains or facilitator to talk to the team about toxic behaviors. Maybe it isn't about just one person—maybe several members of the team engage in behaviors which are not conducive to being the 'winningest' team possible. Ask them to pick one or two things they are going to change as a group and discuss how they will hold each other accountable to that change. Some examples might be: staying out late on game nights, drinking in excess, or bickering during games. Changing toxic behavior is just another step in the creation of a healthy team that knows how to make productive conflict work for them.

Remember, reward the behaviors you want to reinforce. Acknowledge your "bad apple" when she does something emotionally positive. If you pat her on the back only for *athletic* accomplishments, you are likely to see growth in her athletic performance only. If she is usually self-absorbed, not caring about her teammates, and you see her asking how someone is or sharing positive pointers with them, quietly tell her you are proud of her and like to see her showing positive leadership. Reward, reward, reward the positive.

When Talking Doesn't Work

When a toxic person is unwilling to change, it is often not an option to simply remove her from the team. Sometimes you need their talent so much you are willing to overlook the emotional pain and suffering they are causing you and your other players, just to win games. That really isn't fair to anyone. You aren't doing the toxic person any favors by allowing her to get away with that type of behavior, and you are doing a huge disservice to the other members of your team by subjecting them to a toxic environment. In that case, perhaps you need to reevaluate what the player is *bringing* to the team versus what she is *costing* the team.

I have seen toxic players suddenly realize how much more success they and the team could have if she changed her behavior. When that happens, a bad apple can become a strong emotional team leader who can drive a team to achieve amazing heights that one star player could never have reached by herself.

It's possible that you could follow the above steps and not see any change. In that case, some coaches make the difficult decision to sit out, or even cut, star performers. That is never a popular choice, but in the end it can be the healthiest option for the coach, the team, and the program.

If you have tried all the options and see no improvement, it might be time to accept that the toxic person doesn't want to change and your best option is to throw in the towel. I worked with someone who used to say people like that needed to be sold happiness somewhere else: "Things are so bad here. No doubt they are better somewhere else. Please go seek that place." If you are lucky, your toxic person will move on to 'greener' pastures.

Inoculation against Toxicity

While you are spending your time and effort trying to address a perpetually unhappy person, don't forget about the rest of your team. While Pessimistic Patty or Disparaging Donna is working toward change (or toward leaving or being moved on), it is important to keep the negativity from affecting you and your team as much as possible.

The best way to do that is to realize what is happening and deliberately decide not to let her bring you down.

Have conversations with your team about negative behavior and how it makes them feel. Ask them how they recognize when someone is being toxic and how they can avoid the effects of it. Once they are able to articulate it, they will be better prepared to avoid becoming involved in someone else's toxic churn. That is what inoculation is all about. Work toward change on the things you can control, work around or with the things you can't, and do your best to ignore people who wallow in trying to do the opposite. A team that talks about toxicity will be able to power through the negativity until they can eliminate it much more successfully than a team who tries to ignore toxic behavior.

Great Teams are Inclusive, Not Abusive

I stood off to the side watching the last few routines of gymnastics practice. Their coach had confided in me that one of the biggest concerns she had was that the team was splintered into cliques, divided along class lines. She said she didn't understand why it happened every year. Freshmen would seem friendly with everyone at the start, but over the course of the season they would become "cliquey" with only their class. Coach had asked, "Why does every class I bring in act that way?"

Practice ended with the team gathered around their coach. As the coach talked, several team members started removing the athletic tape from their fingers, wrists, knees and ankles. When the group broke, I was surprised to see used tape scattered all over the mat where they had been sitting. A few of the girls stayed behind to pick up all the little pieces and throw them away; those same girls gathered and put away the equipment from practice. They were just finishing when several of their teammates emerged from the locker room, freshly showered and dressed in street clothes. The two groups didn't speak to each other as they passed in the hall.

I asked the coach about the girls who had cleaned up and learned they were the "very talented" freshman class. I could tell she was very excited about their future on the team. I continued the conversation by asking why they had stayed behind to clean up when the other girls had just left. "Oh, <shrug> because they're freshmen. It's been a tradition on this team since before I started coaching that the freshman always pick up after practice. It's kinda like a rite of passage."

I had just discovered at least one of the reasons this team was cliquey: they were hazing.

* * *

Hazing Isn't Harmless

Many coaches and teams disregard what they consider to be "light" or "harmless" hazing. In fact, many people in an athletic environment consider certain activities 'silly team stuff', like: freshman or rookies having to carry equipment, clean up after the rest of the team, sit in a particular place on the bus, or wait to take showers until others have finished. "It's just an athlete thing. It isn't a big deal," they claim. For instance, every year at the start of the NFL season, there are reports in the press of "silly" things being done to rookies: giving them goofy haircuts, making them wear ridiculous outfits, making them carry equipment. The list is endless.

I am going to call it like it is: when an individual or group of individuals is treated as lesser and made to do unsavory tasks or the dirty work that no one else wants to do, it is abusive and it is hazing (no matter how "harmless" it might appear). More importantly, it will damage the cohesiveness of the team. If you want your team to work together as a single unit, they have to view each other as equals.

Address the problem

Take a long, hard look at your team—how do they treat each other? Specifically look at how new members are treated: are there even subtle things that are different? do the rookies wait to get water on breaks? are they expected to behave in specific ways around more senior players? are there humiliating rituals they "have" to perform? are members of your team peer-pressured into drinking or even sex? To solve the problem, you have to notice it.

Have a discussion with your team about the negative ramifications of hazing. Not only is it illegal, it actually damages the team's ability to be a complete unit. Reeducate them about what constitutes hazing.

Many athletes are under the misconception that as long as they aren't using cigarettes to burn each other or tying naked freshman to a tree in the dead of night, they aren't hazing. That simply isn't the case. Your team won't be able to change if they don't understand that treating someone as less important or beneath them is just as bad as other, more obvious hazing rituals.

You can't simply 'outlaw' hazing and expect it to go away. Most universities have anti-hazing clauses that all athletes must sign, but putting their name on a piece of paper doesn't mean they understand what hazing really is or that they won't do it.

A conversation is a great place to start. You also need to provide your team productive, healthy ways to team build (Chapter Nine will give you a great foundation).

As you make the transition from hazing to healthy teambuilding, make sure that you aren't turning a blind eye to hazing. Even an attitude of "It's the janitors' job to clean up; when I leave my garbage on the floor, it gives them something to do" should be nipped in the bud. No one—no matter how good an athlete they are—is so important that they are exempt from treating everyone like human beings and picking up after themselves. The attitude that they are somehow better is a cancer for the team.

MY COMMUNICATION PLAYBOOK

Chapter Nine
Be a Great Leader

Ignorance is shameful only when we have had the opportunity to learn something and rejected it.

–Sydney J. Harris, *Pieces of Eight*

It is impossible to get the measure of what an individual can accomplish unless the responsibility is given (her).

–Alfred P. Sloan, Jr.

I never did anything worth doing by accident, nor did any of my inventions come by accident; they came by work.

–Thomas Edison

* * *

Micromanaging is Bad for Everybody

"I am the head coach here!" Lorrie all but yelled. "I should *not* have to defend myself to my second assistant in front of the team!"

I completely understood her point; her assistant did have habit of second guessing and trying to run the show. I just wasn't sure how much of the current outburst was because the assistant had overstepped her bounds (again) or if it was the head coach's personal insecurity about her authority and her desire to keep a death grip on every tiny detail. But what I *did* know was that it should *not* be taking place on the practice field with 25 athletes within hearing distance.

* * *

Being a micromanager is stressful. Your days are spent worrying about whether things are getting done correctly. "Did the team captain pass that message along like I asked?" "Did my teammate hand in my paper?" "Did the assistant coach send my paperwork to the academic counselor?" "Did the parent's group order food for the tailgate?" If you find yourself worrying about things you delegated, you might be a micromanager. In contrast, if you have someone who is constantly calling, texting, emailing, or asking you about something you are supposed to be doing, someone might be micromanaging *you*.

Let's take a look at both sides of the coin and figure out what the options are for making the situation better for everyone.

Being micromanaged

There is very little that is as frustrating as having someone literally or figuratively looking over your shoulder all the time. It often feels like you have no options but to deal with their constant pestering. Here are a few ideas that might help get her off your back and let you 'do your thing' in peace:

> ***Understand where she is coming from.*** Micromanagement is founded in fear—fear that the mantra "if you want it done right, do it yourself" is true. She is worried that you won't be able to do the task well and that you will make her look bad in the process. *She* doesn't want to fail and therefore doesn't want *you* to fail.
>
> ***Ease her fear.*** It is easy to feel defensive when you think your coach or teammates don't trust that you can actually do an assigned task without their input. Defensiveness isn't going to get you anywhere. Instead, try having a respectful conversation. Start with something like, "I can tell this is very important to you and it's hard for you not to be doing it yourself. What, specifically, do

you need from me to be comfortable that we (important, use "we" to be inclusive) are on the right track?"

Listen to what she has to say and make her feel heard (see Chapter Seven for more on how to do that). It won't do you any good to ask the questions if your micromanager doesn't believe you are paying attention to the response.

Assure her that you will ask for help when you need it. This and the next point seem pretty obvious. However, it is human nature to try to hide when we feel micromanaged. Fight that desire; it will only make things worse. If you have a question or aren't sure, ask! Not doing so will only make the micromanager feel justified in standing over you.

Do a great job. Get the things done you are supposed to do, do them well, and report back when you say you will. Obviously! If you want to be left alone to do a task, you must do it on time and do it right. There is no better vindication than proving that, not only can you do something, but you can exceed the expectations of whoever asked you to do it.

Being a micromanager

Let me guess: *you* aren't micromanaging. No, of course not. You are just 'making sure the task gets done right.' If you are so worried about high quality that you feel the need to constantly check in, ask loads of questions, or spy (don't laugh; I know people who have), then you are micromanaging.

There is no way you can do your job effectively if you keep checking in on someone else. Either you don't have enough to do (I doubt it) or you can't let go and trust them to do what you asked them to do. Here are some ideas for lowering your stress level and helping you become more productive:

Recognize there is* less *work being done when you interrupt to get status. Set reasonable intervals to receive updates. Is it really so important that you need to know exactly what is going on every two hours? Most things don't need to be monitored that closely. Let people report back to you when they reach a milestone or when they have questions. If you absolutely *must* have regular updates, space them far enough apart for something to actually get accomplished in between.

Set expectations about when issues should be escalated. Now would be a great time to follow the steps to getting things done right the first time (later in this chapter). If you create a good plan in the beginning, you will have less to worry about when you are in the thick of things. If people know when to bring issues and problems to you, and that you will help them, they are unlikely to hide things until they explode.

Trust. Yes, yes, I know; this is a tough one. Even if you didn't get to select the people on your team, it is your job to teach and grow them. If you have been effective in that responsibility, you can trust them to do their job well. If you haven't, stop wasting your time micromanaging! Take the time to teach them what you need them to do. It might be a little more challenging up front, but it is the only way to keep your sanity in the long run.

Focus on fulfilling your responsibilities well. I am absolutely certain that *your* To Do's have been neglected if you have been spending your time worrying about everyone *else's* list. Focus on what *really* needs your attention and manage through the guidelines you have in place. It will make the environment much more productive and happier.

Micromanaging is like giving two people the same task—one person to do it and the other to stand there, accomplishing nothing, just watching to make sure it is done right. When that is going on, you and your team are being only half as productive as you could be. Teaching someone how to do something is different than micromanaging. Make it easy for someone to ask you questions, be available to help if they need it, and then trust they can do what you need them to do. It will certainly free you up to do more of the things only *you* can do. Allow your team to soar by taking a step back.

Be a Leader, Not Just a Manager

"You're leading a one-man parade." That is what I used to be told when I was doing something that others thought no one would support. When I was young, that made me think of a drum major in full uniform, head thrown back, marching down a desolate street with a few paper napkins blowing down the pavement—but no one marching behind him and no one watching. The picture in my head always made me laugh. I would think, "How silly for someone to march down the street and not realize that no one was there."

* * *

The idea of a one-man parade still makes me smile. But the sad truth is that many people actually do that in real life. They want to be leaders, but they go traipsing off without checking to make sure people are following. The big question is: How do you become a leader people will follow?

It is important to understand the difference between management and leadership. There is lots of debate about the distinction. Some people say there is no difference and some feel they have nothing in common. For the purpose of clarity, here is how I characterize them:

> *A manager is in a position of power or authority.* We do what a manager tells us to do because we have no choice. Managing is about driving people forward regardless of their desire to go. Anyone can be assigned to the position of manager.
>
> In contrast, *leaders inspire people.* We follow leaders because we believe in where they are going and we want to go with them. Leaders develop and earn their positions; you can't assign someone to be a leader. They either are or they are not. Official leaders have assigned power or titles, but teams will follow an unofficial leader regardless of her actual title.

Lead with a Shared Vision

The first step to being a good leader is making sure the people you are trying to lead have a similar vision to yours. Does your team know where you want to go? Have they been brought into your plan for getting there? If you aren't sure, ask! It is amazing what people will tell you if you give them the opportunity and are open to hearing what they have to say. It is surprising how often "leaders" just assume and don't bother to ask.

Here are some words that come to mind when talking about great leaders:

Passion	Charisma	Integrity
Courage	Honest	Commitment
Trusting	Promote action	Vision
Dream	Rise to the occasion	

Take the time to think about what each word means to you personally. Do you work harder than everyone else because the goal is so important to you? Are you willing to do everything it takes to get there, or do you delegate the dirty work to someone else? What does delegation mean to you? If it simply means making other people do tasks, such as making copies of a flier for the team fundraiser, or setting up cones for practice, you are a manager. If it means asking others to develop solutions and to think about the best way to accomplish what needs to be done (such as brainstorming the most effective way to advertise the team fundraiser or coming up with a creative way to use cones in practice), you are leading.

When you are excited about where you are going, it is easy to regularly check in with your team to make sure they are on board and to use their input to develop a plan to reach mutually beneficial goals. By contrast, if the goals are self-serving and other people are required to help you (because you are paying them, giving them scholarship money, or have something else over them and the only question you ask them is whether they're done yet) perhaps you should think about your use of the word 'leader.' *Being a good leader is going to include management skills, but being a manager does not necessarily involve having leadership skills.*

Interviewing for Fit

Two years ago:

After observing and interviewing dozens of potential players over the course of several months, Coach was positive she had finally found the perfect person to round out her team. The raw talent was there; the passion for the sport was spot on; the girl's high school coach raved about how coachable she was. She was exactly what this team needed to go from 'pretty good' to 'really great.' The school had to recruit her like crazy. Scholarship money was "found" to entice her. Coach even went before the school academic committee to explain that this athlete was *so* good they just *had* to bend the academic standards and accept her. "I promise you won't be sorry. She really is that good." Finally, the athlete committed. The team was so excited to have her that the coaches and players talked about her and the difference she was going to make on next year's stats with their family, friends, and anyone else who would listen.

Today:

I am sitting in the stands watching the team play. Coach's "perfect player" is in her junior season. I have seen her play only a few minutes in a handful of games over the past couple of years; never games that were close or mattered.

I had talked with the athlete when she threatened to transfer at the end of her sophomore year, but she decided to "just stick it out" because she "liked the school." I felt bad for Coach and worse for the player. She did have really good skills, but they never seemed to work with this team; she never clicked. I knew Coach had given up on her and I knew that next season wouldn't be any different. I had no doubt she would end her four years as a college athlete having never played a full game. I felt very sad for someone with so much potential.

I had spent time talking to Coach about it. Coach was right—she *did* have all the technical skills the team needed and she was a driven player, but it wasn't working. The team had never integrated her or her ideas, and her teammates started complaining to Coach about the "perfect" player almost as soon as she arrived on campus. What happened? What did Coach miss? Why did the team treat her like an outsider?

* * *

Sometimes recruiting and interviewing potential players or new coaching staff can feel like a crap shoot. If your luck holds, you will get someone who has the skills you need and fits with your team. If it doesn't, well, then, you end up with an expensive scholarship warming the bench or paying a staff salary while counting the days until the end of their contract.

There are two things that may have gone wrong—one in the interview process and the other when the new team member started—and both are solvable (assuming the team, you, and the new team member are willing to work at it). We will talk about the interview process in this section and how to bring the new member onto the team in the next. It is important to interview someone not only to determine if they have the skills you need, but also to see how they fit with the culture of your team and the larger organization. Additionally, share important aspects of your culture with the interviewee—you don't want them thinking they are accepting a position in the dreamland of Camelot.

To interview for fit successfully, you have to understand your team culture and be able to put it into words. If you have a team communication fingerprint, this will be easy. If you don't, consider how your team interacts. You must be realistic here—it is easy to think about how you *wish* your team was rather than how it *really* is.

When I first start working with a team, I often hear coaches and players complain that they feel like they were victims of a bait-and-switch ploy: "They all acted like they got along great when I was here on my recruiting trip, but at the first practice after I signed on, it was really clear that several players on this team hate each other." "I was told by (the head coach) that he was looking for someone creative who could spice up practice. I was really looking forward to implementing my ideas and making a difference. It turns out that all he *really* wants is a glorified babysitter to make sure the athletes do what he wants them to do."

There is little worse than arriving on a new team only to learn they aren't anything you thought they were—except maybe having a new *player* or *coach* show up who isn't at all who you thought *they* were. Be honest about your team, how you communicate, how you handle conflict, and how the players and coaching staff interact. It makes things much easier when expectations and reality are similar.

Here are a few of the questions I have used successfully during the interview process:

How do you handle conflict?

Tell me about the last time you made a mistake.

How do you set expectations?

How do you like to have expectations set for you?

Do you consider yourself a leader or a follower? Why? (Remember a team needs both.)

What is your leadership style?

What style of leadership is easiest for you to follow?

If a member of your team made a mistake, how would you handle it?

How open are you to adapting new methods?

Do you consider yourself a team player? Can you give me an example of what that means to you?

What types of people do you really enjoy being with?

What types of people do you find more challenging?

Do you consider yourself a strict rule follower or are you more of an out-of-the-box thinker?

You will learn the most if you can ask these questions in an experience-based way. Saying something like "Tell me about a time you had a serious disagreement with someone. How did it end?" will help you learn a lot about the person with one question. Make sure they tell you about *themselves* and what *they* did, rather than about how someone *else* had a problem with *them*. The best type of answers will have several "me" and "I" statements and only a few "they" or "she" comments. Listen for accepting responsibility or placing blame. How does the picture they paint of themselves fit with the culture on your team?

It is important to realize that these types of questions are going to be really different for most people. Young athletes, in particular, are unlikely to have ever thought about things in this way, and you are asking them to think about it under the pressure of an interview.

Don't be overly critical about how the process of providing answers works. Granted, it is data about how your interviewee responds to stress, but it is more important to listen and take notes on the actual answers. There is a saying in the business world, "it is all there at entry." It means everything you need to know is there at the start; you just have to be able to see and hear it. That is exactly what will happen when you ask these types of questions. Everything you need to know about the person will be there—you just have to be able to pick up on it, and that isn't easy. If you are interviewing for a very important role on your team, this might be a good time to bring in some help.

I am *not* saying that anyone who provides answers that don't exactly match your team culture should be out of the running—not at all, particularly if you receive answers that *could* fit or lean in the direction you wish your team would go, or if the individual indicates she is open to adapting to the existing culture. Those types of differences can begin to be ironed out during their first days and weeks with the team (the on-boarding stage; see the next section, below).

However, if you hear a very strong stance that is worlds away from where your team is or where it is going, you might want to make note of them as red flags. Again, that doesn't mean you can't bring the person in. But know what you are getting yourself and your team into. Bringing on a talented bad apple or toxic person (see Chapter Eight) is not going to do your team any favors and it will pull valuable emotional resources away from your existing members. As long as you and your team are willing to deal with that to gain the talent, go ahead and make an offer.

One more thing to remember: sometimes someone who looks perfect on paper, and even interviews well, doesn't fit. Know when to cut your losses and let them find happiness somewhere else. I am not sure it was the right answer for the player or the coach in the opening story for that player to stay—she might have been a valuable asset to a different team, and the coach could have filled her empty spot with someone who was a better fit. Sadly, the player, the team, and the coach will never know.

Bringing on a New Team Member (on-boarding)

I was new on campus and I felt completely lost. It seemed ridiculous to me that no one was willing to help me with what should have been routine things. Where did I have to go to get a student ID? What kind of parking pass did I need? In which lot should I park? Where was the shortcut from the parking lot to the building? Where was the bookstore?

I felt like I was completely reinventing the wheel on everything. I was frustrated and angry. I mean, *really*? As if no one on the team had ever had to do these things? They couldn't just tell me? I started making a list of all the annoying hoops I had to jump through. Next year when the freshman arrived, I would have answers to frequently asked questions ready for them. I hated walking around feeling lost and stupid. I saw no reason why every student who came in behind me had to do it, too.

* * *

Being able to interview someone to determine if they are a good cultural fit for your team is only half the battle. When someone new arrives, they know nothing. They don't understand how your team communicates. They don't know the logistics of getting around campus. And they don't know who the unofficial leaders are any more than they know your offensive strategies. They have to learn everything.

The faster you can bring them up to speed, the more quickly they will be able to focus their energy on being a productive member of your team. The process of bringing someone new into a team is often called on-boarding and is regularly a forgotten component in the teambuilding process.

The purpose of on-boarding is to help a new team member become acclimated to the team culture and become beneficial to the team as quickly as possible. On most teams it looks something like this:

Coach: "This is the team. Everybody, introduce yourselves."

Fifteen or more people rattle off their names.

Coach: "Great, now that you've met everyone, let's get you to orientation."

Right now you are probably laughing because you know it's true. It has either happened to you or you have seen it happen to someone else. That is pretty much all the on-boarding anyone gets; and then we wonder why new members take so long to figure things out.

In order to onboard someone successfully, you need to understand the important aspects of your culture. You should ask yourself and your team the same questions we asked the interviewee while interviewing for fit. If you don't know the answers to those questions, you are not going to be able to explain your culture to someone new. What is your team communication fingerprint? That is something pretty important to be able to explain clearly.

In addition, what are the nuances about your team environment? Maybe the number five key on the locker room code pad sticks. Maybe there is an unwritten rule that the first person in makes coffee and the last person out rinses the pot, regardless of whether or not they drink coffee.

Figure out what the norms are for your team. Think back to when you were new. What were the things you had to struggle to learn? Ask your newest team members. Was there anything that would have made their life easier had they been told up front? It won't be as easy as it sounds.

There are usually lots of little things nobody even thinks about—they just "are." If your team is like most, the only way to learn them is by making a misstep and being chided by the rest of the team—not a very warm or helpful welcome.

In addition to sharing the unspoken cultural norms, there are a few standard questions that everyone on the team is going to want answered:

> *As the new person, what strengths do I have that this team can use right away? How do I stand out in a positive way?*
>
> *Who on the team has strengths that offset my weaknesses? How do I find them and how open are they to helping me learn?*
>
> *Who on the team is going to help me fix a mistake, and who is going to kick me while I'm down?*

Once you have a good handle on your team culture and how the new piece fits into the existing puzzle, you are ready to walk someone through the integration process. Listen if they have questions or concerns. After you think you've covered all the bases, provide them with someone on the team they can go to if something comes up they don't understand. It is always more comfortable to know there is someone in your corner who will help you when you feel lost.

Finally, a few months after someone new arrives, sit down and talk to them about the on-boarding experience. Add things to the frequently-asked-questions list. Continuing to improve your on-boarding process will ensure that new team members are incorporated into the group quickly and as painlessly a possible.

Do you have a story of being 'welcomed' by being tossed right into the fire? How long did you walk around feeling like the newbie who didn't know what was going on? Share it with your team. I am sure your team would love to hear your story, and it will help start the process so your new team members won't feel new for so long.

The Real Art of Teambuilding

Let's start with what teambuilding is *not*. It does not involve blindfolds, ladders, or rope courses. You don't have to toss water balloons, carry eggs on spoons, or pass oranges with your chin. And making everyone wear the same t-shirt does not make them a team. Those are all things you can *do* while you are teambuilding, but they are not going to actually help you *create* a cohesive team.

Real teambuilding involves people actually speaking to each other about who they are as people in order to develop trust. Think about the people you trust. Who are they? Why do you trust them? I would bet you know them really well. You know the kind of person they are, what their talents are, and that they will have your back. How can you create that kind of personal knowledge within a group? Those conversations can take place during activities like rock climbing. But wouldn't it be better if the point of what you were doing was to actually team build rather than get to the top of a rock and hope the teambuilding happens along the way?

When we don't know someone we tend to categorize them by their position. "She is from Texas." "She plays defense." "That's the new pitcher." Not very personal. Start your teambuilding by having the group get to know more about each other. Here are a few examples of conversation starters I have used with teams. But remember, as the facilitator, you have to be engaged, too. Share *your* answers first and the rest of the team will be more comfortable sharing theirs!

What is something about you or important to you that no one on the team knows?

What kinds of things really stress you out?

What is your default response to conflict with someone?

Most people are leaders or followers depending on the situation. When do you want to lead and when do you prefer to follow?

How do you respond to stress?

What is something you are really good at?

What skill do you have that might surprise people?

What athletic skills do you bring to this team?

Of course, there are lots more, but those will certainly get you started. The point is: no one trusts someone they don't know. So help them get to know one another. As each person responds to the question, encourage dialogue about the answer. Ask each other follow-up questions. It is my experience that there are lots of good laughs to be had during a session like this.

If you want to have pizza or brownies or whatever while you do it, great! Go for it—as long as you don't believe it's the *food* doing the teambuilding.

* * *

Have you ever had to engage in a "teambuilding" exercise that was more task than team? Come on, everybody has a horrible teambuilding experience. Share them with each other! I was once involved in a treasure hunt that was supposed to be a teambuilding experience. The team was divided into two teams, each with a list of items to locate and take back to the starting point. The first team to collect all the items won.

One of the things we had to find was a hat. I happened to have brought a hat with me that day. But someone from the other team stole it from me. In my efforts to get it back, I found myself being pinned against a wall by someone bigger and stronger than I was. As I struggled to free myself, I turned my head and my mouth banged against the person holding me. My lip was pinched a little bit, but I didn't think anything of it. It was all 'good fun' in the name of teambuilding—at least that's what I thought until I was called into the office and accused of *biting* my teammate! I was embarrassed and the whole thing was a disaster.

The treasure hunt actually ended up splintering our team into the group that believed that it was simply an accident and the group that believed I had purposely bitten someone. I would certainly recommend against "teambuilding" that creates competition between the people you are trying to get to work together.

Cutting a Team Member

Kylie had always seemed angry. She hated practice; she never showed up for voluntary workouts; she hated the way the team played in games; she hated the starting line-up, no matter what it looked like; she hated having to schedule her classes around practice and often simply chose to take whatever classes she wanted, regardless of scheduling (in fact, the team felt that she picked classes which overlapped with practice on purpose). The coach had pulled her scholarship money the year before (Kylie hated that, too) and often wondered aloud why Kylie stayed on the team at all.

The final straw came when Kylie simply didn't show up for a scrimmage—no text, no email, no call, nothing. Her coach had had it—he made the decision to cut her before the game even started. After the game, he fired off a text, "Don't bother coming back. We don't need someone on the team who can't be bothered to show up to play."

That text started a firestorm. After adding a few choice words about the coach, Kylie forwarded it to the whole team and her parents. She bad-mouthed the team and the coach to anyone who would listen: the Athletic Director, the assistant Athletic Director, the trainer, the academic advisor, other athletes, and her professors. The coach ended up spending untold amounts of time and energy firefighting the drama generated from that one impulsive text.

* * *

Cutting someone is never fun and is rarely easy, but it is one of those things that sometimes must be done. When someone is removed from a team, it always changes the team dynamic. How you move through the process, and then let the remaining team members know, can make the difference between a smooth transition and creating an issue that takes emotional energy away from your team's ability to focus.

Before cutting a player

Brush up on the guidelines. All universities, colleges, teams, and organizations have some sort of policy on involuntarily removing someone from a team. It is very important that you know and understand the process and expectations in that policy. Here are a few things to keep in mind:

> *Requirements for documenting disciplinary or performance-related discussions.*
>
> *Scholarship considerations.*
>
> *What must be said or documented in meetings.*
>
> *What can or should be shared with parents.*
>
> *Does the news need to be announced to the press? If so, how and by whom?*
>
> *What information are you allowed to share with your team?*

Making a clean break

The process of letting someone go is uncomfortable. Many of us are tempted to take the easy way out. But in this case 'easy' is certainly not 'right.' Take these tips into account and you will be much more likely to have a productive conversation with the end result you want:

Schedule a meeting. Cutting a player should be done face-to-face. Not via email, text, voicemail message, or social media of any kind.

This is* not *a negotiation meeting. Be absolutely certain going into the meeting that you will actually cut the player. If you are still on the fence or feel like you would prefer to give her 'one last chance,' it will come across in the meeting. *Threatening* a player with being cut is a dangerous motivation technique—I wouldn't recommend it. Having a discussion about performance is different than actually removing a player from the team. If the player tries to turn the meeting into a negotiation by saying she will change, you must be prepared to stand your ground. Arguing with the player will only make an already painful situation worse for everyone.

It shouldn't be a surprise. If you have done a good job of keeping your players in the loop about your expectations and requirements, no one will be blindsided when you tell her she is not going to be a member of the team going forward. She should be aware when she arrives at the meeting that her eligibility was in question, that her skills were not at the level they needed to be, or that she was on the 'bubble' for making the team. Doing the maintenance of keeping your players in the loop as to where they stand will make the job of letting someone go much easier.

Go into the meeting prepared. Know what you need to say and get to it. A meeting of this type should not need to last more than fifteen to thirty minutes. Beating around the bush or trying to sugarcoat the issue will give the player unfounded hope and increase her stress level. It is important that you be as honest and straightforward as possible.

Remember she is a human being. It might be easier for you to go into mechanical mode and just dole out the facts, but you are talking to a person who has feelings and who likely respects you. Treating her with respect and dignity will help the meeting go as smoothly as possible and keep her from leaving with a bitter chip on her shoulder.

Pay attention to your emotions. Look back at Chapter Six and brush up on self-awareness. If you lose your cool, become defensive, or otherwise don't handle your emotions well, things will go downhill quickly. Being able to keep your emotions in check is important.

Realize you may get a variety of reactions. There is no way to know how an athlete is going to respond to being cut. Tears, anger, acceptance, disbelief (even if they should have known it was coming), feelings of betrayal or humiliation, and confusion are common. Be prepared to accept whatever emotions she feels without judgment.

Close with a positive. Wish her luck in the future. Tell her you enjoyed getting to know her (if that is true). Do not give her false hope by saying things like "you can try out again next year" if you honestly believe there is no way she will ever make the team. Off-handed comments like "it is for the best," "all things happen for a reason," or "this is more painful for me than for you" are shallow and will cause more pain no matter how genuine you feel when saying them.

Avoid gossiping about the meeting. After a stressful conversation, it can be very tempting to blow off steam by recounting the conversation with someone else. Talking to your coaching staff, the trainer, your team captains, or anyone else familiar with the situation is going to be tempting. *Don't do it!* As soon as you tell your side of the story, you open your team up to "Coach said...but former teammate and friend said..." kind of gossip. If you need to release some stress about it, talk to someone outside the team whom you trust (spouse, significant other, friend, etc). Your team does not need a firestorm around the issue.

Talk to your team before you talk to the press. If at all possible, schedule a meeting with your team right after the meeting with the player. However, don't have it in the locker room while the player is emptying her locker—have it somewhere else or wait until she is gone. Remember, dignity is important. After your team is aware of the situation, let the press know, if appropriate.

Telling the team

In so many cases, the only official information a team receives when someone is cut is "Judy will no longer be with us" or "Dannie has decided to focus on her schooling." Or worse, there is no mention of it whatsoever and the team notices a player missing—and whispers of "she was cut" spread through practice. All of these options leave a huge void of information and the gossip mill will take over. You will never see a flurry of texting like what will happen if you cut a player and don't tell your team.

Eliminate the gossip by following these tips:

Know the policy. Existing policy is just as important when telling your team as when speaking to the athlete. Make sure you understand what you can and cannot share. The last thing you want to do is create a libel situation. Even if the policy is that you can't give out any details, you can still be open with your team.

Be as clear as possible. "Annette is not going to be a member of our team going forward. Due to privacy policy and out of respect for her, I cannot go into the details. But I felt it was important to make sure you heard it from me first."

Reassure the team that it was not a random or rash decision. When a team member is cut, your other athletes may worry that they will be next. Reassure them that if you have a concern about their performance, eligibility, or other issues you will talk to them about it before you decide to cut them.

Who will be taking over? Let the team know who will be taking over the vacated role or tasks. Discuss how the team might be different moving forward. If you don't know yet, say so. If you say nothing, the team will feel like you are trying to hide details from them.

Allow the team to process the information and ask questions. It is very important that the team be able to work through any concerns or issues they have while you are in the room. Ask them if they have questions or if there are any ramifications to the player or coach leaving that you haven't covered. You will be amazed how quickly a team will move past the change when you provide them with answers up front.

Realize there will be a period of adjustment. End the meeting by letting the team know that you realize there will be some adjustment, that you expect there to be questions about roles, and that they should be very comfortable coming to you with concerns or ideas. No matter how small a part of the team the former player or coach seemed to be, there will be a hole left by her absence. It will take time for your team to fill it or accept that it exists.

Will you be interviewing for a replacement? This question isn't usually a factor when you cut an athlete. But if the person you let go was a coach, you are going to be looking for a replacement. Keep the team in the loop as you move through that process. Talk to them about what kind of person they think would be a good fit for the team. Let them know where things stand. If it is appropriate, include them in the interview process.

Cutting a team member can be one of the toughest jobs a coach has to do. But too often, very little thought is given to the impact the change has on the team. Spending a few minutes considering how things work on the team, minus the individual you let go, will improve the odds that your team will make a fast, stress-free transition.

Follow the Chain of Command?

My cell phone rang, interrupting my train of thought. I glanced at the caller ID—it was the golf coach I had been working with for the last couple of months. I was surprised—the coach and I had scheduled our semester wrap-up meeting for a couple weeks out because of her very busy schedule and I had not expected to hear from her until then. I tapped my headset to answer:

"Hello?"

"Hey, you got a minute?"

"Sure, I'm just driving back from a meeting. What's going on?"

"I just got out of a meeting with Gerry (the athletic director). He called me in to talk about exit interviews."

I thought to myself, did I know exit interviews were this week? It made sense. It was the end of the year and doing exit interviews with the seniors was normal. I was only working with the coach (and not her team) so I really had no idea what they might have shared with the athletic director. Clearly, the feedback was not what the coach was expecting.

I responded: "How'd it go?"

That simple question opened the flood gates. The coach had done exit interviews of her own with her seniors. They told her everything was great and that she had been a wonderful coach. But when they spoke to the athletic director, they talked about how overbearing she was, hovering during tournaments, and making them nervous when they were on the tee or green. Clearly, the communication lines between the coach and her players were not as good as the coach thought they were. Rather than talking to her directly, or speaking to the assistant coaches about their concerns, the seniors had waited until their exit interviews to complain directly to the athletic director.

I listened patiently as the coach vented. Good thing I didn't have anything else I needed to do right then other than drive.

* * *

Whether you're a coach who has parents going directly to your administrators, or a captain whose teammates take concerns directly to your coach, being the person 'skipped' in the chain of command is frustrating. For athletic administrators, you want to be seen as open and you certainly want to know if there are issues or concerns on a team. However, you don't want every tiny concern on every team brought to you—you'll never get any work done. As the coach, you want to know what is going on with your team before you get blindsided from the top.

So what can you do? For starters, make sure you know what you expect from your chain of command. In your mind, when is it okay for someone to skip a link in the chain? Once you have some concrete ideas about what would work for you, talk to the people above and below you on the chain. What are *their* thoughts on how issues of link-jumping should be handled? Getting everyone on the same page will eliminate misunderstandings and feelings of betrayal.

Indirect reports can be more challenging. If an academic advisor hears about a problem from a student-athlete, should she take it to the assistant athletic director or back to the coach? Again, setting expectations upfront is going to be key. When everyone knows how information is supposed to flow, it is less likely that misunderstandings will result from personal interpretation.

Parents, coaches, and athletic directors have the added challenge of the student-athlete involved. Parents want what they believe is best for their child; the coach's job is to make the team successful; and the athletic director (AD) needs everything to work smoothly.

One of the best lines an athletic director and his assistant can learn is: "have you talked to your coach about that?" Without it, the AD's phone will ring off the hook and a line will form around the office. Additionally, coaches should make a point to develop open communication with parents. It is amazing what a difference it makes when a parent simply feels like the coach is listening to them.

When the chain of command gets broken

There are always at least three people involved when the chain of command gets broken: the person doing the breaking, the person skipped over, and the person skipped to. Let's take a look at all three positions:

Being the person skipped to

Let's assume you have created the expectation that the chain of command should be followed and you have someone who is insistent that it should *not* apply in their case. Here are a few things you can try to address the situation:

Push back on them to use the chain of command. If people get solutions from you when they don't follow the rules, they will have no motivation to follow them the next time they have a problem. Ask them if they have used the process—if not, they need to; if yes, why do they feel like it didn't work? Often people will go over someone's head because they didn't like the answer they received rather than because they didn't receive an answer at all.

Have them put their concern and what they believe to be a viable solution in writing. Having someone write out a problem will help them become really clear on what their issue is. Then, if you do have to sit down to talk with them, they won't waste your time just venting.

Have a meeting with all of the parties. In this case, you are likely to have to wear the hat of facilitator. But getting all the information out in the open at one time is a lot better than an ongoing flurry of emails, phone calls, and visits. In-person is best, but a conference call is also a good an option.

Meet one-on-one with the person who has the concern, if you feel it is appropriate. Be careful not to jump to any conclusions—you are only hearing one side of the story. Put a time limit on the meeting and be prepared to wrap it up by letting them know what the next steps are. Letting them leave without a clear understanding could lead them to go over your head, too.

Regardless of which path you take, it is important to always ask the complainant for a solution. It is not your responsibility to have all the answers. Plus, understanding their thought process for getting to a solution will tell you a lot about the nature of the concern.

Being skipped over

It is very frustrating to get an email or phone call from your boss telling you that someone who should have come to you with a concern has gone directly to them. If you are fortunate, you have a boss who has followed the steps above. Even if you don't, there are some actions you can take:

> ***Assess why they didn't come to you first.*** Is it a case of their not liking the answer they got from you? There isn't a whole lot you can do about that. If they simply didn't come to you at all, why might that be the case?
>
> Perhaps they felt like you don't really listen or the environment isn't safe to talk to you. Take a look back at Chapter Seven and see if there are areas you could improve. If it is appropriate, ask the person why.
>
> ***Talk to your boss.*** Have a conversation about why he or she thinks the chain of command was broken and how things can be handled better next time.
>
> ***Accept that sometimes people just break the chain of command.*** Sometimes there really isn't anything you can do about it. There are people who are always going to want to go directly to the top. That is out of your control. The best thing you can do is have a good relationship with your boss so when it happens it isn't a big deal.

When <u>you</u> want to break the chain of command

Sometimes it feels like there really is no option other than to go over someone's head. Before you do so, there are a few things to consider:

> ***What do you expect to accomplish?*** It is important to know what you want as an outcome. As I noted above, the person you are talking to is likely to ask you for a solution.
>
> ***Why are you breaking the chain of command?*** Do you feel like you can't talk to the correct person, or have you tried and gotten nowhere? Or is it that you just don't like the answer you received?
>
> ***Is it an option to request a three-way meeting instead?*** Your relationship with the person you are "skipping" is going to be much better if you include them in the process rather then cut them out completely. If you feel like you aren't getting (or can't get) what you need directly, then having a meeting with all three people in one room might be a good option.
>
> ***Provide feedback.*** After the situation has been sorted out, you have an opportunity to make the process better. If it is possible and appropriate, provide your experience to the person who was "skipped." She may be open to making changes to reduce the chance that someone goes over her head in the future.

Having and using a chain of command seems like it should be pretty clear, but there is often a feeling that taking things directly to the top will get faster action. Creating transparent expectations for raising concerns, and having a planned procedure in place for when those expectations are not met, will save lots of time and aggravation for everyone involved.

Do Things Right the First Time

Katelyn looked like she was about to cry. "I wasted *so* much time" she lamented.

I looked at the pile of color-coded notes. They were impressive and I had no doubt the information in them would have led to a great paper. Unfortunately, Katelyn had misunderstood the assignment, and most of the research and work she had done wasn't really relevant.

I picked up the assignment and read it. I wondered if our time would be best spent going through what she already had to see if we could apply it or if she should just scrap it all and start over. I hated to think about the amount of rework she was going to have to do, but there might be no way around it.

* * *

How many times have you or your team started working on something only to realize you were headed in the wrong direction? Not only is all the time you spent wasted, but in some cases you actually have to spend *more* time *undoing* it so you can start again. Maybe you thought you understood, but didn't; maybe you actually *did* understand, but the requirements changed and nobody told you. Whatever took place, it is frustrating, annoying, and not good for anybody when it occurs.

The very simple (and I think trite) answer you hear to this problem is often, "make sure you understand the requirements up front." Well, yeah, that isn't rocket science. But how? None of us goes off half-cocked on *purpose*.

I am going to share several questions you can ask yourself, your coach, a professor, or your team in any situation. Individually, they are not particularly earth-shattering. As a group, if you take the time to get solid answers to each of them, I can guarantee you will spend less time firefighting and being reactive, and more time being productive and proactive.

Do I understand the specific expectations of this project or assignment (i.e. do I know the end goal)? Have I articulated my understanding to the person in charge and received feedback so I know I am correct?

Do I understand the path the leader (captain, coach, professor, etc.) expects to be taken (i.e. do I know the plan)? Do they care how I get there or only that the end product is what they want?

Do I have a clear understanding of what success looks like to the leader (i.e. will I know when I am successfully finished)?

Do I know where this project or assignment falls on the priority list, who has the authority to change that priority, and how I will be notified if it changes?

If requirements or other details about the project change, how will I know? Do I know how changes will be communicated? Is there an email list I should be on? Will I get a phone call or is there a website I need to check regularly?

What if I have a problem? Is there an agreed-upon plan in place so I know when and how I should escalate issues or concerns?

Have I communicated my understanding of the above information to the leader and received his or her agreement that we are on the same page?

Have I communicated the above information to my team or group and listened to and answered their questions and concerns?

I can almost hear you thinking, "It would take a lot of time to gather, and then disseminate answers to all of those questions." I will grant you it might take a day or two and a few emails or phone calls to make it happen—but it is all information you will need to be successful. It is better to know up front rather than discover it after you have been working toward the wrong goal for a week or longer.

If you feel like you are constantly chasing your tail or putting out fires, take the time to ask and get answers to these questions. It will make your life much easier, help manage your time more effectively, and avoid the frustration of having to backpedal and re-work things.

MY COMMUNICATION PLAYBOOK

Chapter Ten
Get More from Your Potential

Destiny is not a matter of chance, it is a matter of choice; it is not a thing to be waited for, it is a thing to be achieved.

–William Jennings Bryan

The thing that is really hard, and really amazing, is giving up on being perfect and beginning the work of becoming yourself.

–Anna Quindlen

Never let the fear of striking out get in your way.

–Babe Ruth

If we all did the things we are capable of doing, we would literally astound ourselves.

–Thomas A. Edison

There is nothing wrong with making mistakes. Just don't respond with encores.

–Anonymous

* * *

Prepare, Perform, Evaluate

Each and every one of us has to perform every day. Whether you are doing a presentation for class or trying to raise your team to victory in a game, you are performing. Your teammates and your professor or coach are expecting something incredible. You don't want to disappoint. Doing your best is the only option.

You start by preparing: you gather facts; run an extra mile; put together the best PowerPoint ever or watch more film; maybe you even stand in front of the mirror to give yourself a pep talk about how well prepared you are or that you are the best person for this job. You go to bed the night before imagining handshakes and high-fives after a successful performance. You've *got* this. You are the woman!

The Big Day finally comes. You are confident and ready; there is no doubt in your mind you will be successful. But then it happens: you make a mistake. The professor asks a question you can't answer; you miss an easy pass; the turn or jump you were supposed to make didn't work like it did in practice; the presentation is missing a slide. Everything starts to go downhill.

You try to focus on not making mistakes, but you feel your chest get tight. Suddenly you realize, "Oh no! I'm *choking*! I was so *ready*. I did everything right. I even stood in front of the mirror! I am so *stupid*! How can I be failing?"

All that preparation and potential: wasted. You couldn't get it together when the pressure was on. You will never trust yourself to do another big presentation. The coach realizes you can't handle the pressure. Your teammates put their hands on your shoulder, shake their heads, and say, "Next time. You'll get it next time." You just want to crawl into the nearest crack and hide. You don't believe there will ever *be* a next time.

* * *

So what happened? Clearly the knowledge, skill, ability, and preparation were there. Why did you choke? I can tell you why: *evaluation during performance*. It will kill you every time, in every situation, no matter what you are trying to do.

Evaluation means you are analyzing something to determine what worked, what didn't, and where you can make changes to improve. It is absolutely necessary in order to reach your full potential. However—and this is big—you can *only* evaluate something *after* it is over, *not* while you are doing it. Your brain can only do one or the other at any given time—perform or analyze—*not* both.

The Seven-Second Rule

Here is what I teach clients: use the seven-second rule. Praise yourself or kick yourself for seven seconds, then let it go. If you don't have seven, take two. The point is, get over the highs and lows quickly so you can focus on the task at hand. The next shot, the next slide, or the next opportunity is the only thing you can control. Leave the past in the past. This takes practice, and it often helps to have someone who can catch you as you begin to evaluate yourself.

I am not saying you can't make adjustments—of course you can, and should. But adjustment is different than evaluation. To make an adjustment you simply think, "That didn't work, I'll do something different." An evaluation sounds something like, "That was stupid. Why did I do that? I should have..."

'Should' is useless *during* a performance. You can't do anything about 'should'—it is over and done, so stop *should*-ing on yourself. Worrying about what just happened, and what other people think, will only derail the rest of your performance. Take a deep breath, say, "that was awful" and move on. After you nail everything else and you get to have those high-fives and pats on the back, you can watch the tape to figure out what happened during that one moment of collapse and use it during your next preparation.

If you find yourself thinking back to a previous mistake, say to yourself (out loud if it makes sense), "Not now! I will evaluate that later." Bring your mind back to the moment at hand. Focus on what you need to do next. What pitch are you going to throw *next*? How are you going to take the ball away from your opponent at *this* moment? What are the points on *this* slide that need to be explained? Teaching your mind to stay in the moment is critical to all types of performance success. *You can't practice and prepare* while *you perform*. Evaluation and critiquing don't work while performing, either.

Have you experienced *'should*-ing' during a performance—either from yourself or your coach? Maybe you "choked." What was going on in your head as your 'A' game went out the window? It could be a great example to share with your team to start a conversation about the difference between evaluation and performance. Understanding it is the first step to being able to successfully separate them and perform to your potential. Talking about it with your team will get you started on the path to peak performance!

Recognizing and Managing Burnout

Taylor was a bubbly, outgoing lacrosse player in the middle of her freshman season. Even though she was young and relatively new to the team, she was quickly becoming an unofficial team leader—her teammates, coaches, and teammates' parents loved being around her. She hadn't been a starter yet, but she had played long stretches in several games. Everyone thought she was the up-and-coming player who would carry the team to greater heights over the next several years.

I was shocked when she walked into my office unannounced, dropped her book bag on the floor and said, "I think I'm going to quit the team."

I gave her a quizzical look and asked, "Are you not happy here? Are you thinking about transferring?"

She shook her head, "No, I'm done playing lacrosse. I'm tired. My body hurts every day when I get out of bed. I have too much class work to do. I don't have time to see my friends. I haven't spoken to my sister in two weeks, and I just failed an exam. You know what my grades looked like last semester. If I fail any classes, I won't be eligible to play anyway."

I was looking at a classic case of burnout. Taylor was clearly overwhelmed and jumping to the one thing she thought she could control: playing or not playing lacrosse. I knew she didn't *really* want to quit: she was an athlete to the core and happiest when she was playing. She just needed to understand she had more control of her life than she was giving herself credit for, and that she had the power to organize things so they *worked for her*, rather than running around trying to make things work for everyone *else*.

* * *

In today's competitive environment where there is always someone looking to take your spot in the starting lineup or happy to take over your role on the team, burnout is common. Athletes with minor injuries nurse them in rehab instead of participating in practice; coaches who wish they could call in sick for a "mental health day"; athletes and coaches alike quit because they just have no more to give.

To deal with burnout, those solutions fall right in line with the common suggestion of taking a break or making a change in your routine. But burnout is caused by something deeper than boredom or overwork. Taking a break or eliminating responsibilities might be a short-term solution, but to *really* solve burnout, you have to understand *why* it happens.

What Causes Burnout?

Burnout is caused by being held accountable for things outside of your control. Being held accountable means someone believes you are responsible for outcome—that 'someone' could be you, your professor, your coach, your boyfriend, your parents, your friends, anyone. In addition, control (or the lack of it) could be more perception than reality.

In the business world, there is a saying, "responsibility without authority." In the abstract, this can be a bit challenging to understand so I will give you a physical example. Imagine you are responsible for building a brick wall, but you have no authority to purchase the mortar you need to hold the bricks together.

Without mortar, there is no way you can build the wall, but at the end of the week your boss is going to yell at you because it isn't done. Imagine how frustrating that would be week after week. Having the *responsibility* to make something happen but not believing you have the *authority* to make the decisions that will allow you to be successful can lead to a serious case of burnout.

If you are dealing with burnout, you may find it helpful to do an assessment of your responsibilities: work, home, community, church, athletics, school, anywhere you have someone expecting things of you. Write everything down (and don't forget important things like sleep).

Put them in order of importance—knowing how things are prioritized will help you determine where you can make changes. Things that directly affect your health have to be on the top of the list—you can't cut out eating and sleeping.

Ask yourself these questions:

> *Who has this expectation: me or someone else?*
>
> *Is it a reasonable expectation? Could the expectation be altered to be more manageable?*
>
> *Do I have to do it, or could it be delegated or declined?*
>
> *Do I have the authority to be successful?*

There are always responsibilities that can, and should, be shifted to someone else; there are a few that don't actually need to be done at all; and there are several where the accountability and control don't match (one or the other has to change: more control or less accountability). Those are the places to start having the tough conversations if you want to be successful.

The bottom line: The only thing you can be held accountable for is doing your best, every time. What that looks like compared to someone else is not within your control. If you give 75% but your competitor has a bad day so your performance was better than theirs, is that success? If you give everything you've got but their performance is superior, is that failure? If your answer to either or both of those questions is 'yes,' you can bet you are headed for burnout. You can only control *you*—not *you compared to* someone else.

Sometimes Good is Good Enough

We live in a fast-paced, pedal-to-the-metal, give-110% world. Perfectionism is the norm and anything less than all you've got isn't going to get the job done. But we know there is no way we can live like that all the time and in every facet of life. There have to be times and places when good really *is* good enough.

I took a 300-level biology class when I was an undergrad. It was a big class (some counts were upwards of 500 students; I don't know if it was really that big, but we'll go with that number). The professor was teaching his own theories and was known to be a stickler for details. I went to all the lectures, watched the recordings he posted on his website, participated in chat boards, and studied like crazy. I even gave blood for extra credit.

At the end of the semester, I had 989 out of a possible 1,000 points. You have to admit that is overkill, but the worst part was that he ended up grading on a curve. Anyone with more than 560 points got an "A." He showed a bar graph of all the points in the class. My 989 was close to 200 points more than anyone else in the class. In retrospect, I clearly could have spent a little more time on my social life and a little less on biology.

But how could I have known? The signs were there—I just didn't bother to pay attention enough to pick up on them. So how can you know when you don't have to drive yourself crazy trying to be perfect?

* * *

Fortunately, there are several things within your control that you can do to make sure you are giving your best while not killing yourself to be perfect all the time:

> ***Set priorities***. What is most important today? Notice I said 'today.' Your priorities change—maybe as often as daily. Some days your family is going to be most important and on other days it may be school, your team, or your health. Make time for the top priority to be you. If you know where you need to focus, you will be able to delegate or put on hold other things. You can't give 100% to

everything every day, but you can prioritize and average out to that "A" in most things over the long run.

Which expectations really matter? I certainly believe in the saying 'under-promise and over-deliver.' However, if an assignment is due in two weeks and you pound away at your computer for 15 hours a day to turn it in early, you're probably over-doing it. If delivering something early gains you nothing, delivering it on time is good enough. Know when things are due and estimate how long it will take you to do them. Then lay out each task to make sure they are completed to an acceptable level by the day they are due.

Give yourself a break. I read a blog the other day that said, "I can't do something I don't love for the rest of my life just because my Mom told me to." So who told you everything has to be perfect all the time? Go have a conversation with that "ghost," because they are wrong and it is stressing you out. If a 92% will get you the same A as a 100% will, how much stress is that extra 8% worth? Do you really need to stress yourself out over something that is really of no consequence?

When the time comes that you do need to step up and give that 110%, do it! You know you have it in you, and you will call on it when you need it. If you are always running with the throttle wide open, you won't have anything left to give when you hit that bump in the road.

Become a recovering perfectionist. While you are at it, keep in mind that expecting other people to always be perfect will only lead to disappointment. Create expectations that are reasonable, communicate them clearly, and then go out and attain your goals.

The bottom line: *good is good enough when 'great' doesn't gain you anything.* I would have gotten the same "A" in that bio class with only 561 points. The extra 428 points were useless. I couldn't carry them over; they didn't show up on my transcript and help me get in to grad school. I gained nothing from those points—except being able to tell this story. In that case, good certainly would have been good enough.

Ambiguity Kills Performance

It was a beautiful spring day. An assistant coach, Claire, and I had decided we could talk just as well on a walk around the cricket field as we could sitting in an office. As we walked, she told me about her frustration when the head coach forwarded emails to her as well as the other assistant coach with no instruction.

I asked if the content of the emails was enough to determine who should be doing what. Claire laughed, "Sometimes they are just FYI; sometimes I am supposed to do something; and sometimes Monica (the other assistant) is supposed to handle it. It feels like we are *all* working on *everything* and so *no one* is really working on *anything*."

* * *

Have you ever been involved in a situation where it was not clear what you were supposed to be doing, who was in charge, or how decisions were going to be made? When you don't know where you are going, who is leading, or what the path looks like, you are likely to end up somewhere you don't want to be. It's not at all surprising, but we have all been in situations where time has been wasted milling about, not being productive, or worse: creating something that isn't needed.

Role ambiguity

As leaders, we often fail to spend enough time considering who is doing what. Teams with role ambiguity never get out of the storming stage of team development where some responsibilities are being covered by more than one person while others languish undone. Role ambiguity can affect any member of a team. However, it is often a relevant issue for players who are red-shirting or who are injured because their roles within the team are usually left undefined and change throughout the season.

An additional area to be aware of is the coaching staff. You don't want them wasting time tripping over one another because they are trying to accomplish the same things. Thankfully, solving this problem is easier than you might think:

> Start by creating a comprehensive list of the tasks your team needs to accomplish, then ***put them into categories by how often each task needs to be done***;
>
> Next, ***consider which tasks build on each other***. Does it make sense to have the same person be responsible for all of the pieces? Maybe a handoff of information or a team effort is required;
>
> Finally, ***reflect on the individuals who make up your team***. Who is best suited for each of the tasks? Does everyone have a specific role they are responsible for filling?

Once you understand the tasks, how the work should flow, and how your teammates fit, you will be able to assign clear roles to each team member. Don't forget to revisit your lists when team members or tasks change. This is not something you can do once and expect it to work forever.

Goal ambiguity

Do you understand where your team is going in the long run? All too often, we plod through our daily grind in the fog of many 'little things' that need to get done. Take a step back and look at the overall picture.

What *exactly* are the long-term goals of your team? How does that fit into the overall plan of your organization? Will the way you are going about your daily routine actually get you to those goals? Does your team understand how the things they are required to do fit into the larger picture? Being able to answer those questions and make changes has the power to improve your team's performance very quickly.

Decision-making ambiguity

Very little will bog a team down faster than not knowing who is making decisions or having only one person responsible for the entire decision-making process. I have volunteered on teams and been frustrated by the amount of time everyone spent accomplishing nothing because no one was making decisions. Have you empowered your team to make decisions so they can continue moving forward even when you aren't readily available, or do you expect them to come to you for every little thing?

Imagine a shortstop who wasn't allowed to make important decisions. With runners on first and third, one out, and a hit coming toward her, should she ask the coach what to do? No, of course not! The shortstop knows enough about the game to quickly consider the situation and make a decision. Your team is no different. Coach them well, give them the power to make decisions, on and off the field, and make it clear when they need to come to you and when they should go for the double play on their own.

Plan ambiguity

What are your expectations of how your team should go about reaching team goals? The answer to that question is directly dependent on how well you have defined roles, goals, and decision making. When everyone knows where they are headed, who is doing which tasks, and how decisions are being made, the path is clear.

You may not have to lay out a detailed plan—it's likely that your team is capable of coming up with the most efficient, effective plan on their own. However, if you have a specific path you want them to take, don't leave them in the dark about it. It might be clear to *you* that there is only one "right" way to reach the goal, but they might not see it. So, if you have a route laid out, share it. If you trust your team and are giving them creative license to craft the best plan on their own, let them know. Teams and individuals are most productive when expectations are clear.

Worrying Damages Productivity

I was sitting in the stands watching the last few minutes of a soccer game when the mother of one of the athletes sat down next to me. I smiled and commented on how well the team was playing. She agreed and then fell silent for a moment. I was just starting to feel a little odd about the silence when she said, "I'm worried about Mack."

I knew Mackenzie had red-shirted the year before due to a leg injury. She had been given medical clearance to play in the off-season and had worked like crazy to be in condition when she arrived at camp. I had not spoken to her directly, but she seemed to be doing pretty well.

I turned toward her mother and replied, "Oh?"

"She is much more timid on the field than she used to be and she seems to worry about *everything*," her mother clarified.

I wasn't sure which part of the conversation to follow first. Several thoughts ran quickly through my head: playing timid was a matter of opinion; anxiety could definitely affect her performance. I wondered how she would feel about her mom talking to me.

I returned my focus to the conversation as her mother continued, "She worries so much that she's sick to her stomach most days. She worries about school work; the situation with her roommate; if she is eating enough or too much; if she will ever be able to play at the level she was before she was injured; if she will get injured again; if her teammates think she still belongs on the team; if they will bring in a freshman to replace her; about her boyfriend leaving her; if the internship she has is going to give her the experience she needs..."

Mom continued the list of various concerns and anxieties she thought were affecting Mack's game. If Mack was half as upset about things as her mother seemed to think she was, it certainly could be a distraction on the field. But it could also be that her mom was blowing things out of proportion. I wouldn't know unless Mack came to talk to me.

* * *

A little bit of worry will actually *improve* performance. It makes you study for exams, keep track of project due dates, and do extra practice drills. But *too much* worry can inhibit your ability to sleep, keep you from focusing, and cause performance to plummet.

Fortunately there is something you can do about useless worry:

> ***Notice that you are worrying.*** This may seem elementary, but it is not uncommon for anxiety to become such an expected (and accepted) part of life that we don't even notice the symptoms. Do you have tightness in your neck? An ongoing ache in the pit of your stomach? A general feeling of tension? Difficulty focusing on one thing at a time? You are likely worrying.
>
> ***Pinpoint your worries.*** What, exactly, are you concerned about? Try to be as specific as possible. Rather than saying simply "school," determine what it is about school that has you worried.

Do you not understand the material? Are you afraid of making mistakes? Do you feel like you have so much to do there is no way you can do it all? Maybe competition days stress you out—are you afraid you will fail? What, exactly, is the concern?

Write concerns down. This might seem counter-intuitive, but making your worries concrete will help you with the next steps.

Are your worries within your control? In other words, is there something you can do about them? I have a friend who worries incessantly about his mother's health. He can certainly encourage her to take care of herself, but the choice is hers—he has no control over her actual behavior. Things like time management, getting extra tutoring, or seeking help for performance anxiety are within your control—whether or not a professor gives a pop quiz, or an opponent is faster than you on a given day, are not.

Create two lists. Make one list of things you can control and the other of things you can't. Label them "Within my control" and "To worry about later." It is a waste of time and energy to worry about things that you do not have control to change.

Gather more information. Ambiguity and the unknown are big worry-monsters. The more you know, the better you will be able to make decisions. How often does that professor actually give pop quizzes? What does it take to be ready for them? Who could tutor you in calculus? (Take another look at the *Ambiguity Kills Performance* section, above.)

Create a To-Do list. The things within your control can always be broken down into smaller pieces. When you feel overwhelmed and don't have enough time, break the project or activity down into the individual tasks you need to do and estimate the amount of time you will need to do each. Once you have that information, you can start to schedule things, get them done, and mark them off the list.

Start making progress. The best thing you can do about worry is take action. Do one small step at a time and mark it off the list.

Add new worries to the proper list as they come up. When you catch yourself worrying about something on your "later" list, remind yourself that it is on the list and that you don't need to concern yourself with it right now.

If you find yourself with nothing to do and worry-free, pick up your "later" list. Is there anything on there worth spending your happy mood on? I think not.

Worry is a normal human condition. Just make sure the bridges you are building are ones you actually need—worrying about things you can't control, or that will never happen, is like building a bridge to nowhere that you will never cross!

Name the Dragon

A few years ago, I attended a week-long seminar aimed at understanding group dynamics and how individual personalities create a team culture. At the end of an intensive seven days, we were asked to inspire one another by writing comments on sticky notes. One of the notes posted under my name read, "You are more than a match for the dragon."

On the four-hour drive home I wondered, "What dragon? What does that mean?" I have decided that it means the person who wrote it believes I have the ability to overcome the obstacles life sends my way. I believe that is true of most people—but you can't overcome an obstacle until you *know* what it is. You have to *name* the dragon.

* * *

It sounds simple. How hard can it be to figure out what is standing between you and the success you desire? In reality, it can be more difficult than it appears. Many of us get so caught up in our day-to-day tasks that we ignore the things that are keeping us from reaching our potential. Here are a few thought-starters to help you focus on where you want to go and what is keeping you from getting there:

> ***Choose one area in your life*** (school, athletic, civic responsibility, work, family, personal relationships, your health, etc).
>
> ***If you could create the perfect outcome, what would it look like?*** Don't be afraid to dream big. Be very specific. Take notes as you create the picture of perfect success.
>
> ***What is impeding your progress toward that success?*** Maybe you believe you don't have time. Are you afraid to try? Do you lack the ambition to start? Are you allowing someone to hold you back? Be really honest with yourself. This is about you, not about what someone else is doing.
>
> ***What are your 'controllables'?*** If you want better grades, things like learning good study skills, getting a tutor, and meeting with the professor are within your control. If you want someone special in your life, you can control meeting new people and showing them your real self. If you want to be a better leader, you can learn how to be inspirational so people will follow you. All of us have choices we could make which would change our direction or circumstances—what are yours?
>
> ***Why aren't you controlling those 'controllables'?*** What is keeping you from doing the things that will lead to success? Finding these answers may take some self exploration. Talking through your thoughts and ideas with a trusted friend or a professional can help. That 'why' is your dragon. Maybe you believe the consequences will be too great. Maybe you would rather let other people control

things so you have someone to blame if it goes wrong. Ignoring the dragon or choosing not to fight it doesn't mean it doesn't exist—it just means it is controlling you.

Repeat the thought process on a different area in your life. You might be surprised to learn that you have one dragon holding you back in lots of areas or maybe you have multiple dragons ganging up on you. Once you realize that, you can separate them out into manageably sized battles.

Determine where you want to go and what you need to do to get there. When you figure out why you aren't doing those things that will give you success, you will have a name for your dragon—it will no longer be just a scary beast, hiding in the mist. You can start putting together a plan to fight it. You are more than a match for the dragon.

Slay the Dragon

When I ride my bike along the canal, I often allow my mind to wander to whatever topic it feels I need to think about. I have developed and practiced presentations and considered the direction I want to take my business, but most often I find myself thinking about my clients, their struggles, and how I can help them.

One particular day, a freshman discus thrower was on my mind. She had a stress fracture and was struggling with having the motivation to do the rehab the trainers had assigned. I wondered about that. She was a motivated athlete; prior to her injury she had trained with focus and determination. I knew she wanted to be a champion. Something had her doubting her ability to rehab and it was keeping her from even trying.

That was a dragon I was going to have to help her slay.

* * *

It is easy to become overwhelmed with the responsibilities of life—particularly if you experience a setback. It can feel like every time you turn around there is something else demanding attention. Sometimes that feeling is called 'trying to move a mountain with a teaspoon'; others have referred to it as 'trying to eat an elephant.' But mountains and edible elephants seem rather passive to me.

Challenges and hurdles rarely feel like they are just sitting there waiting to be conquered—it feels like they are fighting back, trying to keep us from our success. The picture in my head isn't of me sitting with a spoon in my hand moving dirt; it is one of me dressed in full armor, sword raised, ready to take on whatever is standing between me and victory. So in keeping with the dragon analogy, the process of figuring out what is standing between you and success is called "Name the Dragon" while dealing with and overcoming those barriers is aptly named "Slaying the Dragon."

When you recognize you have your back against the rocks and fiery dragon breath all around, having the skills to continue the battle can be a lifesaver:

Recognize when the dragon is getting the best of you. People who feel like they have too much to do and too little time can be found at either extreme of the 'busy' spectrum. They will either be involved in a constant flurry of activity, jumping from one task to another without actually finishing anything, or they will be at a complete standstill, unable to even figure out where to start. Noticing when you are in one of those places is the first step to getting out.

Create order in the chaos. When we have lots to get done, our brains often throw constant "reminders" at us because we are worried about forgetting something. But trying to keep track of things in our head hampers our ability to focus on the task at hand. I know that making a list sounds mundane and time consuming, but having everything on paper will allow you to prioritize and organize each item individually rather than look at a nebulous mass of demands and figure out what to do next. Creating a list is well worth the time spent.

Create and fill buckets. Family, friends, work, school, athletics, social, community, etc. Life always has buckets. Figure out which ones apply, and put the tasks that belong together in the same bucket. It is also helpful to put the buckets in order of importance. If you had to choose only one bucket, which would it be? What if you could have two? This is about you and what is important to you—not about what other people want you to do.

Which priorities belong to whom? Once you have tasks in buckets and the buckets prioritized, it is time to figure out which tasks are most important. Don't forget to consider why a certain task has priority. Is it important to you, or is someone else in your life demanding that it be a priority? I am not saying one should necessarily have more weight than the other, I'm just saying that understanding where the pressure is coming from is relevant.

Create smaller pieces. Take the top priority from the most important bucket and break it down into individual tasks. For example: getting to practice on time might include laundering your practice gear, locating your cleats, packing a snack, purchasing sports drinks, and filling the car with gas. Individually, each task is manageable. But put them all together ten minutes before you should be walking out the door and they are overwhelming. Do this breakdown for the first one or two priorities in each bucket.

Create a timeline. Determine when each priority needs to be done and back-track to figure out when the small tasks that make up the priority must be accomplished. Combine small tasks that make sense to be done together (go to the bank, get gas, and buy sports drinks all in one trip, for instance).

Dig in. Start plugging away at those small tasks. And don't be afraid to ask your teammates for help—sometimes fighting a dragon is a team effort. It is amazing how quickly doing simple tasks will add up to a big project getting completed.

Pat yourself on the back. Don't forget to notice your progress. Cross things off the list as you finish them. Be proud of yourself for moving forward.

Repeat. Maintaining a running list of priorities that have been broken into tasks will help keep you on top of things and keep the dragon from growing into that overwhelmed feeling that creates stagnation. The bonus is that, once you have a list, it doesn't take a lot of time and effort to continue using it.

I have often said my life feels like I am fighting seventeen dragons at once and I can only wield my sword for so many hours a day. I can spend all day fighting one dragon or I can take on a small battle with each dragon and make a little bit of progress against each of them—each day the choice is mine. As long as the dragons are being fought, and I remember to notice the progress, I can be happy.

Learning how to slay a dragon one small battle at a time is a skill you will use for a lifetime. It also makes for great team discussion. Talk about the dragons you face as a team and how you can start winning the battle. It is great for teambuilding and will make a positive difference in your success.

Dealing with Distractions

Brianna stormed off the court visibly furious. She jerked out her mouth guard and growled to no one in particular, "Did you *see* that call? I didn't *do* anything! Someone *bought* that ref! I've *never*...." I couldn't make out any more of what she was saying as she stomped toward the water cooler. Several minutes later, she was standing behind the bench, still venting—mostly under her breath. I knew her coach wanted to put her back in, but was waiting for the rant to end in order to lessen the risk of Brianna saying something to get herself ejected from the game altogether. I wondered how her teammates where dealing with the distraction of Brianna's torrent of negativity. It just might be the topic of discussion the next time I was to meet with the team.

* * *

The human element is a factor every athlete has to deal with at some point in her athletic career. It might be a referee making a bad call, a fan or parent yelling something distracting or even hurtful from the sidelines, or trash-talk from the opposing team.

Here are a few techniques you can use to keep a distraction from disrupting your ability to perform up to your potential:

Before the presentation or game: prepare

Know your triggers. What really sets you off during a competition? If someone fouls you and gets away with it, does it send you off the deep end? Do you let your opponents push your buttons? Pinpoint what gets to you so you can be ready to counteract it when it happens.

What is your default response to those triggers? How would you like to respond instead? Remind yourself that what other people do is outside your control, but you have control over how you react to them.

Have a strategy to bring your attention back into focus. You might take a deep breath or touch your pinky finger to your thumb. You might benefit from visualizing the negative incident (along with the emotion tied to it) being put into a box to be stored in a corner of your mind for later evaluation. Create an anchor that stops the progress of your destructive response and reminds you to stay in the moment.

Create team vocabulary (see Chapter Seven, *Creating a Team Vocabulary*) that you can use to bring yourself or a teammate back into the moment. It may also be helpful to let your teammates know what cues to watch for so they can use that vocabulary to help you.

During the presentation or game: perform

Repeat to yourself that you cannot control someone else, only your own reaction. If you allow their distraction to interfere with your ability to give your best, they win. Focus on the specifics of what you need to do in that moment. Allow your mind to settle into the technique of what you are doing and to block out the crowd noise or an opponent's banter.

Recognize your default response and consciously change it to the response you want. Catch yourself going down the wrong thought path. Force your mind to come back and go in the direction you want it to go.

Use your strategy. That is why you developed it!

If you have the luxury of time, ***implement The Seven-Second Rule.*** Allow yourself to be really annoyed for seven seconds. Really focus on it. Is that as annoyed as you can get? Come on, I know you can be more annoyed than that! Jump up and down, scream if you need to. Then let it go.

Focus on the very next thing you need to do. The next ten seconds are the only ones that matter. Make each ten-second segment as perfect as possible, and you will perform flawlessly.

After the presentation or game: evaluate

How did you do? If you have video, watch it with a critical eye. Where did you get distracted and how did you handle it?

How did your focus strategy work for you? Were you able to bring yourself back to the moment? If yes, keep using that strategy. If no, decide if you need to continue to practice to get better at it or if you need to find a better anchor.

Did you notice that certain types of distractions are more likely to affect you than others? Practice staying on track in spite of those particular things that distract you the most.

Repeat

Keep using your focus strategy and anchor until they are second nature. Having a go-to strategy that you know works for managing distractions during competitions isn't something you are going to stop using when you stop playing—distractions come up all the time in everyday life. The strategy you perfect now will serve you well long into the future

Learn to not get distracted. Everyone gets distracted. The only difference between a great performance and a derailed one is how the distraction is handled. The good news is that performing at your peak without being distracted is a learned behavior. You can do it if you put your mind to it and your team is willing to help you.

MY COMMUNICATION PLAYBOOK

Chapter Eleven
Bonus Topics

Courage is resistance to fear, mastery of fear, not absence of fear.

– Mark Twain

You will miss 100% of the shots you don't take.

–Wayne Gretzky

You can't think and hit the ball at the same time.

–Lawrence Peter "Yogi" Berra

Let us not bankrupt our todays by paying interest on the regrets of yesterday and borrowing in advance the troubles of tomorrow.

–Ralph W. Sockman

* * *

Passing the Torch

A college coach I knew used to hold an annual team meeting to elect captains. Conversations were lively around what the team needed in a captain, what the role entailed, and who would be the most successful. The outgoing captains weighed in with their thoughts on the role and what it took to be successful in it.

After the list of candidates was created, a vote was taken by the coach. The vote was held by a raise of hands with the athletes' eyes closed as each candidate's name was called. Every year there was chatter after the vote that it was 'odd' how the coach's top choice always seemed to win.

One year, it was leaked by the new captain that the coach actually didn't take the vote into account—the coach knew who he wanted to be captain and, regardless of the actual vote, the winner was always his preferred candidate. The fallout and backlash from the team learning of this deception was tremendous. At the end of that season, the coach was out of a job.

* * *

Your team is finally clicking: they have figured out how to use productive conflict to their advantage; they are performing to their potential and beyond; it feels like success comes easily. Then your most advanced team members, the ones the team counts on in tough situations, graduate and move on with their lives. Contracts are up and members of the coaching staff pursue other opportunities. It is time to pass down the leadership torch.

For many teams, the rotation of athletes happens like clockwork, while changes in coaching staff are more rare. In either case, maintaining momentum and retaining team knowledge are crucial. So what can you do to make sure the advances in communication and productive conflict the team has made don't get lost?

When your most senior players leave, you are losing more than just headcount and on-the-field talent. They are also the most knowledgeable about the team culture; they are, most likely, team leaders; and they are certainly a component in team stability and structure. If their departure is not managed correctly, your team is likely to revert back to the storming stage of team development and, with it, to the drama. But with good planning and team involvement, you will continue clicking along without a problem:

Plan early. The time to think about this type of change is not two weeks before someone leaves. The better you understand how your team functions emotionally, the better prepared you will be to adjust to the loss of key individuals—and that takes time. Start now, and then update the information anytime you make personnel changes or observe that your team culture has evolved. Consider what roles the team members fill both on and off the field. Ask your team to think about how the structure of the team will be different without those players or coaches.

Who is/are your second-in-command? These people are likely to be your emotional leaders. They may not have a leadership title (yet) but their thoughts and ideas hold power with the team. You need them to step up as the team changes. Are they aware of the role they need to fill? Is the team prepared to follow them? This is not a role you can assign—emotional leaders step up because it is who they are and the team is happy to follow them.

Do you have any power-hungry individuals you need to watch? A team in transition is vulnerable to what amounts to a hostile takeover. When key players leave, a leadership vacuum can develop if plans are not in place to fill it. A self-serving individual will notice and exploit that weakness. Your best defense against it is being aware.

What role is going to be vacated? What exactly do the people who are leaving do? Not just the position they play or the tasks they complete: what emotional roles do they fill? Are they the person who notices when someone is a little "off" and checks in with them? Do they make sure that the lines of communication on the team stay open? Maybe they notice when conflict is brewing and make sure the team addresses it. It is much easier to find a replacement when you know exactly what void needs to be filled.

Involve the outgoing individuals. Nothing gives new leadership authority like an endorsement from the exiting leader. If it is possible, include them in the discussion about how the change will be made and who is taking over. When the outgoing members feel they are leaving the team in good hands, the team will have more faith in their ability to move forward with continued success.

Notice I used the word "discussion." Bring the whole team in and talk about what is happening. Pretending the team isn't going to be affected is just that: pretending. Take their thoughts, ideas, and desires into account. They are going to have the best understanding of what it means to have specific people leave. When the whole team is involved in the conversation and feel part of the transition, it will be much more seamless.

What if you can't wait for them to leave? On more than one occasion, I have been involved with teams that have a player, or even a coach, who was so divisive that many members of the team were counting the days until she was gone. If you are coming out of a season with that kind of animosity, having a conversation about passing the torch from the outgoing team members to the next leaders may be difficult, if not impossible. In those cases, it may serve the team better to have a restructuring meeting after the complexity of a toxic senior has been eliminated by graduation. You will know which option is best for your team.

Having a key team member leave can be a perilous time for any team. Manage it well, and it will hardly be noticed. Manage it poorly, and your team may backslide into confusion. If you have examples of past teams who have struggled to make the transition from outgoing players to new players, talk about it.

What happened? Why didn't it work? What can this team do differently? If you have had teams who never missed a beat, why were they successful? It is certainly possible to hand off power in a smooth, organized manner—you just have to put some thought into it.

A Team's Worst Nightmare

The most devastating loss imaginable has nothing to do with an opponent on the court, on the field, on the pool deck, or anywhere else. Every year there are tragic stories of players who make the winning shot or walk off the practice field only to collapse and die. There are those who become involved in an altercation or have a car accident and are killed. Coaches have coached a winning game then died of a heart attack the same night. The stories are more common than anyone would like and each and every one is a devastating tragedy for their team.

* * *

When a teammate or coach passes away, most universities offer school psychologists to the team. In my experience, that means a statement such as "counselors are available." The responsibility to take advantage of that counseling is usually left up to the individual students to find time in their schedules, contact the counseling center, and make their appointments. If they don't take the initiative, they miss out on the benefits of having the counselor available. I hope many students take it upon themselves to get the counseling they need.

There should also be some time set aside by the coach to talk with the entire team about what the loss means to the team as a whole. It is in this team meeting that many coaches and their administration risk missing the boat. Consider these suggestions and questions to assist a team through a tragedy so they can come out a stronger and more unified team. If I know anything about athletes, I can say for certain that those who have passed would want that for her team.

Bring in a specialist. It is imperative that the coach bring in a specialist to work with the team. Expecting each young woman to seek out help on her own is not acceptable. Additionally, if they are all working through their grief alone, or even in small groups, the team will develop fissures and cliques.

Accept that dealing with grief is an ongoing process. Dealing with a trauma is not something you can do once and expect everyone to move on. Accepting the loss and dealing with the grief will take time. Tributes and vigils can be a wonderful way to show support. Assuming the team trusts the grief specialist, that specialist should check in with the team regularly—maybe once a week. The team will know when they are in a good place and able to support themselves.

How do your athletes deal with strong emotions? That brings us to some important questions. Was this team ever given the skills to talk to each other about strong emotions? Do they trust each other enough to be open and real? Is their team environment safe enough for a team member to drop the 'tough athlete' facade and say, "I'm not okay"? Will the team respond with support or expect a 'game face'?

When some are ready to move on and others aren't. At some point in the future, there will be a player who has been able to move beyond this heartbreak. She will think in her mind, "Yes, what happened was awful. But it has been long enough. It's time to move on." What happens if that teammate actually voices those thoughts and her teammates aren't there yet? Does your team have a strategy to have a conversation so fraught with emotion?

Coaches must grieve, too. Finally, the coaching staff is going to be the example the team follows. Don't be afraid to grieve with them. Putting up a tough front for the team and grieving in private will make them think they're expected to do the same. Their minds will make up things like, "Coach doesn't really care." "Coach doesn't understand us and how hard this is." "We aren't allowed to be emotional." "We have to be tough." Sharing with your team will help the team trust you even more.

I am sure your team is resilient and determined. I know you will come through the loss. It is my hope that the community and your coaching staff will provide them with the support and guidance they need to do more than just make it through—you have the opportunity to become a better team for the loss and pain. If even one good thing can come from a life pointlessly cut short, don't you owe that to your fallen teammate?

MY COMMUNICATION PLAYBOOK

Section Three

Helpful tools to assist on your path to becoming an excellent communicator.

The Seven No-Fail Secrets to Stop The Drama!

Seven tips to help anyone have more effective conversations, develop the use of productive conflict, and *Stop The Drama!*

The Nine Secrets to Great Teamwork

Nine tips created to help a group of individuals become a team that knows how to work together toward greatness.

Feeling Words List

Feeling words to help you put your internal dialogue into words. If you can't find the right word for how you are feeling, you are never going to be able to explain it to someone else.

What a Good Communication Program Looks Like

A short outline to assist you in developing a communication program for your team. If you know what you are looking for and what you are trying to create, you are much more likely to make it happen.

Example Contract

Some teams have found it beneficial to have a written contract to help them use productive conflict instead of drama. This is an example of what yours could look like.

Glossary of Terms

Some of the terms in this book might be new or unfamiliar to you. The glossary is provided as a quick reference guide to assist you.

The Seven No-Fail Secrets to *Stop The Drama!*

Speak from the "I." Own your stuff. No one can "make" you feel anything. You get to choose.

Allow yourself space to feel. Don't let a conversation run away with you. Feel your emotions and label them before words are flying out of your mouth.

Put your internal dialogue into words. You cannot expect someone to behave as if they know what is going on in your head if you never tell them, no matter how "logical" you think it is.

Assume the positive. Most people are not out to 'get' you. You and your teammates all want to be successful. Believe everyone has a positive reason for what they are doing or saying, even if they aren't doing it very well.

Ask before providing feedback. Nobody likes to be blindsided. If you have a concern, set the foundation for a positive discussion.

Create and use team vocabulary. Create phrases or words that everyone understands in a given context. Many miscommunications happen because words provide less than 10% of the meaning of the message.

Know when to call an emotional time-out and do it. When a conversation gets to the point where it is doing more damage than good, take a break. Set up time to talk about it again later. Be careful to never let a topic get pushed under the rug and 'forgotten.'

The Nine Secrets to Great Teamwork

Set expectations. You cannot expect someone to meet your needs, or the needs of the team, if you never tell them what those needs are.

Hold each other accountable. If someone isn't pulling their weight, ask them what you can do to help them step up to their responsibilities.

Support each other (check in). Know what each of your teammates looks like when she is stressed and how she likes to be supported. If you are not getting what you need from your teammates, *ask!*

Care enough to give the tough feedback, and trust each other enough to apply it.

You cannot observe how someone is feeling. Only the external symptoms of feelings can be observed. Realize that your interpretations of those symptoms might be wrong.

It is impossible to observe 'why.' You can see *what* someone does and *how* they do it, but never *why*. To know why, they have to tell you. Never just make up 'why.'

Play brave, not afraid. Trying and failing is better than doing nothing.

Never evaluate *during* competition. Adjust and move on. Stay in the moment. Perform when you are performing and save evaluation for after the game when you can do something about it.

Celebrate and remember successes. Learn from, and move past, disappointments.

Feeling Words List

Happy	**Afraid**	**Excited**
alive	anxious	alert
cheerful	apprehensive	connected
delighted	desperate	cooperative
ecstatic	fearful	curious
elated	frightened	eager
energized	insecure	energetic
exuberant	intimidated	engaged
fortunate	nervous	enthusiastic
gratified	overwhelmed	inspired
joyful	panicked	involved
loving	scared	open
optimistic	shaken	optimistic
pleased	terrified	ready
satisfied	unsure	stimulated
thankful	vulnerable	thrilled
	worried	

Unhappy	**Confident**	**Frustrated**
alienated	accomplished	aggravated
crushed	capable	annoyed
defeated	competent	confused
demoralized	confident	dissatisfied
depressed	determined	distressed
disappointed	effective	helpless
disheartened	encouraged	hindered
distraught	hopeful	irritable
drained	perceptive	irritated
empty	positive	let down
gloomy	proud	pointless
hopeless	secure	restless
lousy	self-reliant	stuck
miserable	strong	suffocated
sorrowful	successful	uneasy
submissive		uptight

Calm	**Angry**	**Embarrassed**
blasé	agitated	ashamed
careless	betrayed	bewildered
collected	bitter	disgraced
composed	disgusted	foolish
content	enraged	humiliated
easygoing	exasperated	hurt
indifferent	fuming	idiotic
lackadaisical	furious	insulted
laid back	hostile	insulted
levelheaded	mad	let down
mellow	offended	mocked
nonchalant	outraged	mortified
peaceful	provoked	offended
relaxed	resentful	teased
relieved	upset	uncomfortable
	used	

Tired

apathetic

checked out

detached

disengaged

drained

empty

exhausted

fatigued

jaded

numb

shut down

sluggish

stressed

vulnerable

weary

worn out

What additional words can you add that apply to *your* unique situation or team?

What a Good Communication Program Looks Like

A good communication program will:

- Have a facilitator trained in team development;
- Have regularly scheduled meetings;
- Be customized to the specific needs of your team;
- Provide a framework of behavioral communication skills;
- Create a common language for your team and the coaching staff;
- Provide a standard method for addressing and resolving conflict; and
- Provide a standard method of giving and receiving feedback or criticism.

A successfully developed, taught, and practiced communication framework will:

- Increase team problem solving;
- Increase team accountability;
- Increase team trust; and
- Improve team cohesion.

These changes will lead to:

- Better team performance;
- Less energy spent on team "drama";
- Increased interpersonal skills;
- Fewer problems which need to involve coaches or administrators; and
- Better communication across the scope of life interactions.

Example Contract

I, ______________________________ (name of athlete/coach) of the ______________________________ team, understand the damage that gossip, backstabbing, cattiness, and other drama do to me personally and to the potential of my team. I agree that I am committed to using *The Seven No-Fail Secrets to Stop The Drama!* to address and deal with disagreement or conflict with my teammates and coaches. I further agree that I will use *The Nine Secrets to Great Teamwork* to get the most from my potential and the potential of this team for the __________ (year or spring/fall) season.

This includes, but is not limited to:

I will not personally engage in firestorming with or about my teammates;

I will bring up concerns, issues, disagreements, or problems when they are small;

I will leave resolved issues in the past;

I will love my teammates enough to tell them the truth; and

I will trust my teammates enough to use the truths they tell me.

____

Printed name

____

Signature

____

Date

Glossary of Terms

Brainstorming: Getting all the possible solutions (no matter how silly they may seem) on paper without judgment or critique.

Checking In: That act of asking someone how they are and offering assistance if needed. Should happen every time an athlete comes off the field, out of the pool, finishes a competition, when someone looks visibly upset, etc.

Communication fingerprint: The way an individual communicates; what she finds funny; how she handles disagreements. As variable as personality or dialect. See also, Team Communication Fingerprint.

Conversation maintenance: Making a point to verify what is being said; is the same as what is being heard. Should be done as both a speaker and a listener.

Drama: Any action or behavior that negatively affects the team or team members, i.e. gossip, backstabbing, catty behavior, grudges, mean-girl actions, ostracizing, cliques, negative personal interactions, screaming, ugly messages on Facebook, maliciousness, unkind texts, etc.

Emotional bullying: Attacking a person's reputation; alienating them from their friends; telling lies/starting rumors; exclusion; taunting; harassment. Also called "mean-girl" behavior or emotional bullying; relational aggression.

Emotional intelligence: Understanding and expressing your emotions effectively. Being able to correctly interpret the feelings of others and respond to them appropriately.

Emotional leader: The individual on a team who is in tune with the moral or emotional temperature of her team. If she is happy, the team is happy; if she is not, the team is not. This individual will often seek out her teammates to check in with how they are doing and offer emotional support.

Emotional time-out: Taking a break from a conversation that is getting out of control.

Feedback: The information provided to someone with the intention of helping them improve.

Firestorming: The swirl of building emotions and drama created on a team when everyone is talking and pointing fingers about something while no movement is being made toward a solution.

Forming: The first stage in Tuckman's stages of team development. Individuals strive to be accepted and avoid conflict. Also see storming, norming, and performing.

In-groupness: The feeling of being a member of a group that shares confidences and trust in opposition to people outside the group or members of a different group. 'Us' vs. 'Them.'

Inoculation: Preparing someone for a potentially negative or difficult situation by having a discussion about what to expect. Example: "Be prepared for Coach to push us really hard the first week of practice; she always wants to find who has the work ethic to be on this team."

Internal dialogue: The thoughts, ideas, and feelings that take place in an individual's head during a conversation.

Mean-girl behavior: Attacking a person's reputation; alienating them from their friends; telling lies/starting rumors; exclusion; taunting;

harassment. Also called emotional bullying, relational aggression, emotional bullying.

Norming: The third stage of Tuckman's stages of team development. Individuals begin to function as a team with most members understanding their role and where they fit on the team. Also see forming, norming, and performing.

On-boarding: The process of bringing someone new on to an existing team. Orientation; showing newbies the ropes; teaching them the team culture. Often done very poorly: 'thrown into the deep end', 'baptism by fire', 'tossed to the wolves.'

Performing: The final stage in Tuckman's stages of team development. The team is functioning smoothly at the highest level. Everyone knows her role and there is no unproductive conflict. It is not unusual for teams to revert back to earlier stages after reaching the performing stage due to changes in personnel or leadership. Also see forming, storming, and norming.

Playing brave: 1) Not accepting mediocrity as a way of avoiding failure (if you don't try, you can't fail); **2)** The willingness to stretch outside your comfort zone to reach your full potential. Only achieved when athletes trust that their teammates will be there to help them if they stretch a little too far.

Productive conflict: The act of addressing and handling a disagreement or misunderstanding using an established set of healthy communication guidelines which lead to resolution.

Relational aggression: Attacking a person's reputation; alienating them from their friends; telling lies/starting rumors; exclusion; taunting; harassment. Also called "mean-girl" behavior or emotional bullying.

Result: The outcome of a conversation or series of conversations.

Storming: The second stage in Tuckman's stages of team development. Individuals begin to confront each other about how the team functions and who is responsible for what. This stage is particularly uncomfortable for anyone who dislikes conflict. Many teams become permanently stuck in this stage or revert back to it when change occurs. Also see forming, norming and performing.

Team communication fingerprint: A developed and agreed-upon framework for how a team approaches disagreement, conflict, and expectations. Can be specifically designed or come to be organically. May or may not be healthy.

Team development, stages of: A model for group development proposed by Bruce Tuckman in 1965 and commonly used in the business world to describe the function of a team. "This team is stuck in the storming stage." Or "I really miss being on a performing team." Also see forming, storming, norming and performing.

Trigger: The point or moment when a conversation goes from being nothing important to being something that requires maintenance, monitoring, or control.

Unofficial leader: Members of a team who influence the direction or decisions the team makes without an official title such as Captain.

About the Author

As a young athlete, Robyn often wondered why girls were so mean to one another. She couldn't wait to get out of high school and into the real world where she expected people to act like grownups—but it didn't take long to learn that even among adults, women don't treat each other very well.

After fourteen years in the corporate world, she was able to attend college to pursue her passion of helping people achieve more from their potential. She received a Bachelor of Science in Psychology (Summa Cum Laude and Phi Beta Kappa) from the State University of New York at Stony Brook; then her Master and Doctor of Applied Organizational Psychology from Rutgers, The State University of New Jersey, with a concentration in Performance and Sport.

On her way to receiving her degrees, Robyn observed the many ways in which team sports and business teams mimicked each other in how they failed to succeed because of poor communication and non-productive conflict. She realized that high school and college student-athletes could benefit from the same skills taught to high-level executives in large corporations, and that executives could benefit from knowledge gleaned from sport psychology. Because those skills are not offered across the sport-business boundary, Doc Robyn developed the strategies you see here.

Recognizing this niche needed to be filled, the newly minted Doc Robyn started her business, Champion Performance Development, to provide sport psychology skills to the corporate world and executive coaching skills to the sports world. She also founded the *Stop The Drama!* campaign to share her knowledge with young women who, like herself, have a passion to achieve more from their potential.

Currently based out of central New Jersey, half-way between New York City and Philadelphia, Doc Robyn travels internationally to share her message with those who have a passion to succeed. She shares her passion for contributing to the success of women (and the men who interact with them) by speaking at colleges, high schools, corporations, and events, encouraging people to take the *Stop The Drama!* challenge and holding *Stop The Drama!* events.

Doc Robyn can help <u>your</u> team!

Doc Robyn speaks to a variety of audiences of men and women around the country: coaches, student-athletes, administration, corporate, student bodies, and nonprofits. Her most requested presentations include:

Stop The Drama!

Why do people communicate the way they do? Old methods used to be effective, but now they only limit our success and make us miserable. Doc Robyn will provide you answers and share tips that your group can use right away to have more effective communication, engage in productive conflict, and achieve more from your potential.

The 411 on Team Conflict

All teams have conflict—even the great ones. How conflict is handled determines if a team grows through it or is torn apart. Does *your* team know how to engage in productive conflict so problems can be resolved and put in the past? Or are you making the mistake of letting them flounder in the dark when it comes to team problem solving? Be proactive! Have Doc Robyn arm them with the skills they need to be successful now and in the future!

Remarkable Leaders, Not Just Managers

Anyone can be assigned the role of manager. "Get that done." "Have your people do this task." "Keep track of the project's hours." "Don't go over budget." Only the great have true leadership prowess.

Don't cheat existing leadership potential by making them figure out the difference between being a passionate leader and simply being a manager! Doc Robyn will provide knowledge, skills, and abilities in an interactive and enjoyable way that will make a difference.

If you liked what you read...

...get your own copy of *Stop The Drama!* or get copies for friends and colleagues who can benefit from its wisdom and spur their teams to new heights! Discounts are available on bulk orders.

...learn how you can take the *Stop The Drama!* challenge, invite Doc Robyn Odegaard to speak to your team or organization, inquire about attending one of her events or learn about discounts for ordering books in bulk.

...visit one of Doc Robyn's websites:

www.StopTheDramaNow.com

www.ChampPerformance.com

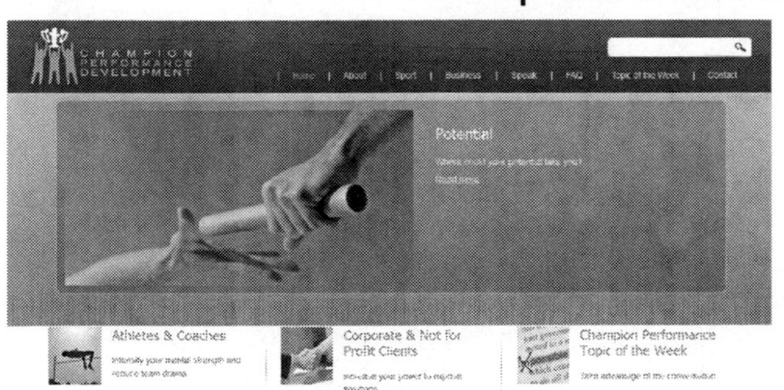

…join Champion Performance Development, the *Stop The Drama!* campaign, and Doc Robyn on Facebook, Twitter, and LinkedIn:

www.facebook.com/ChampPerformance

www.facebook.com/StopTheDramaNow

www.Twitter.com/DocRobyn

http://www.linkedin.com/in/robynodegaard

CPSIA information can be obtained at www.ICGtesting.com
Printed in the USA
BVOW011622120412

287528BV00005B/61/P